COOKING FOR TWO

COOKING FOR TWO

Marshall Cavendish London & New York

Edited by Yvonne Deutch
Designed by Eddie Pitcher

Published by
Marshall Cavendish Publications Limited
58 Old Compton Street
London W1V 5PA

ISBN 0 85685 377 1

Printed in Great Britain

INTRODUCTION

Everyone who has ever struggled to adapt a recipe specially created for four will appreciate the timeliness of – and the necessity for – a book which concentrates on easing the burden of *Cooking for Two*.

Instead of the frustrating struggle involved in trying to halve an egg, or the higher mathematics implicit in estimating an obscure fraction of a teaspoon, there is a whole breathtaking (and mouthwatering) selection of recipes quite definitely for two. The traditional standbys of the two-person household, such as steaks and hamburgers, are not forgotten, but in addition there are those recipes once thought to be the sole preserve of larger families such as roasts, whole chicken dishes, soufflés and crêpes – all appropriately scaled down in size or with suggestions to use the 'leftovers' creatively. And all of the recipes are easy to cook and absolutely guaranteed delicious to eat.

Supercook's *Cooking for Two* will provide the modern cook with hours of browsing, cooking and eating pleasure.

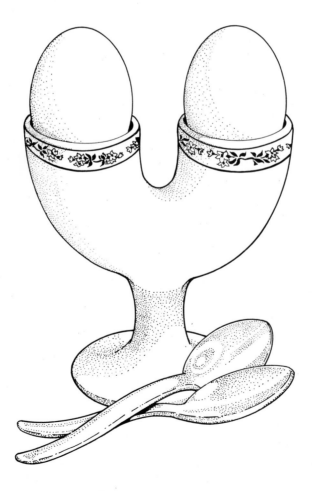

CONTENTS

PLANNING FOR TWO

How many times have you tried to cook a meal for two, only to find that every recipe that you read is intended for four or even six people? It is extremely frustrating to have to halve, quarter or even 'third' the ingredients listed, and of course such items as eggs resolutely refuse to be divided. Yet, when you think about it, some of the most important meals are for just two people: the relaxing dinner for the parents when the children have gone to bed; everyday meals for the older or retired couple; tasty suppers for the urban 'professional' couple; romantic dinners for young (or not-so-young) lovers; down-to-earth meals for apartment sharers on a budget – all these occasions are becoming much more traditional than a massive family gathered around the dining table.

It is for these and many other similar occasions that this book has been specially written. Here are recipes for all contingencies, from the panic-stricken emergency to the long-planned special occasion. If you envy the wide range of materials and scope of menus available to large families or hostesses who entertain on a grand scale, read on and discover that the more intimate meals that you require need not be restricted or predictable. In fact your best policy is to take a really positive attitude towards cooking for two – for example, there are far more opportunities for you to indulge in some luxurious treats from time to time – two can afford steaks more often than four.

PLANNING

There's no getting away from it, before you embark on a successful career of being the best cook-for-two in town, you must reconcile yourself to the fact that imaginative *and* economical meals call for a very high degree of organization in the kitchen. You need to know which items can be profitably bought in bulk, and which ones can't; which foods keep and for how long; how to create different dishes from the same basics; how to put the leftovers from one meal to good use in another. Native ingenuity (and low cunning) will help solve some of these problems as they come up of course. But you can, in fact, avoid most of them entirely by common sense. And that means planning your meals ahead.

Take meat for example. Many families of two never have a roast – simply because it doesn't seem worth buying a large and costly joint of good roasting meat for just two people. Or is it? Maybe we can learn something from the Victorians whose vast joints served the entire family from Sunday to

Friday inclusive, like the old recipe for vicarage mutton: hot on Sunday, cold on Monday, hashed on Tuesday, ground on Wednesday, curried on Thursday, and broth on Friday. Even with modern refrigeration that's asking a bit much for two people. All the same there are many splendid recipes that call for cooked meat – as you'll see from this book. So why not have a proper roast on Sunday and get at least two more imaginative meals from the same piece of meat. It's just as economic as buying three, separate, smaller items.

Equally important for the busy cook are the advantages of cooking ahead. To prepare two or three casseroles or cook-ahead dishes at the same time actually takes very little more time than preparing just one. And, of course, some casseroles and curries actually improve in flavour after a day or two and then being re-heated. While you're preparing meat, always remember to put the bones into a stockpot with a few vegetables and herbs and some seasoning to make a fine rich stock. With the advent of the instant stock cube, this lovely culinary art is dying out – a sad state of affairs, for nothing can replace true home-made stock. To feed the neighbourhood dog with the bones, and deny yourselves this traditional luxury would be a total surrender to convenience cooking.

BUYING
One of the basics of cooking for any number of people, not just two, is to use fresh food at its peak condition, and as well in season as possible. Almost all meat, fish, cheese, fruit and vegetables are bought by weight, so you can buy exact quantities when and as you need them. With fresh foods, you must learn by experience how not to over-buy. One lettuce is usually too much for two on one day. Therefore it needs to be stored in an airtight plastic container in the bottom of the refrigerator. So many fruits and vegetables are conveniently sized for individual servings; potatoes, aubergines (eggplants), apples, oranges, avocados, melons and grapefruit to name but a few, can all be stuffed and prettily served in their own skins. Buy salad ingredients on a small scale - half a cucumber, a few tomatoes, a small lettuce – this will ensure freshness and variety. However, not everyone can depend upon having fresh food available all the time, so here are a few tips on buying ahead and storing your produce.

Fortunately canned foods and most packaged foods come in varying sizes. Do remember to buy in smaller sizes. There is nothing worse than having half a can of peaches or tomatoes mouldering away in the darkest recesses of the refrigerator until it simply has to be thrown away. However, even for two, buying some items in jumbo sizes or large quantities can save money. For example good olive oil works out much cheaper (sometimes about half the price) if bought in half or one gallon cans. Kept in a cool, dark place it will stay in excellent condition.

There are some things which obviously should not be bought in large quantities – eggs, coffee (which rapidly loses its fragrance even in bean form) and salad vegetables, are prime examples. On the other hand, rice, cereals, flour, sugar, and pasta are worthwhile bought in bulk, and should be stored in airtight jars or tins. If you're cooking with wine, and propose to drink some with the meal as well, it makes good sense to buy one of the litre bottles, so you have enough both for cooking and conviviality. Try to buy those bottles with plastic fitted caps – when you've used the quantity you need, simply snap the cap back on, and the wine should keep adequately for a week. Of course, since there are only two of you, you'll sometimes be able to afford an occasional 'special' bottle or half bottle of a really excellent wine.

STORAGE
Naturally, in the end the quantities of food you can buy depend on how long they will keep and what storage facilities you have at your disposal. If you are the proud owner of a deep freeze, you have few problems. However, a large freezing compartment in the refrigerator is quite suitable for two – but do take proper notice of the maker's recommended storage times for frozen foods. Your freezer allows you to make up food in large quantities, and to store it in two-serving portions. You save on fuel bills this way and can also take advantage of bulk food bargains. Do buy one of the excellent publications on freezing that are widely available; you'll be delighted at the practical and imaginative hints for using this modern miracle.

An obvious candidate for freezing is ice-cream. Even if you have an ordinary refrigerator with a frozen food storage compartment, ice-cream is easy to handle. Try making your own – the flavour is breathtaking compared to the commercial brands, since you use only the best ingredients (see the recipe on page 13).

REFRIGERATOR STORAGE TIMES
The biggest single source of waste of fresh foods is caused by overstocking – and the following basic list of average refrigerator storing times should help you avoid any major disasters.

Meat: Meat is very expensive, and should never be wasted. All meat should be put into the refrigerator, after being wiped and wrapped in foil, immediately after you get home from shopping. Large pieces of meat will keep up to five days, steaks and chops rather less, bacon slightly longer; cooked meat will keep from three to five days if kept in an airtight container.

Fish: This is a much neglected source of protein, and there is an amazing variety of both freshwater and sea fish to choose from, many ideally sized for two people. Fish should be eaten as fresh as possible, and whether cooked or uncooked, within two days at the most. For frozen fish, consult the star ratings on the refrigerator, and keep it in the freezing compartment.

Poultry: Fresh poultry, drawn and wrapped in foil will keep up to three days, as will cooked birds if placed in the refrigerator as soon as they have cooled. Frozen ducks, turkeys, chickens etc. should be kept wrapped, in the freezer, or for not more than two days in the main body of the refrigerator.

Vegetables: Salad vegetables such as lettuce will keep up to four or five days in an airtight container in the bottom of the refrigerator. Greens will stay fresh for up to a week in the vegetable compartment. For frozen vegetables, follow the manufacturer's instructions.

Cheese: Hard cheeses are best stored in the main body of the refrigerator, wrapped in foil, but they should be taken out a few hours before use. Soft cheeses should only be bought in the exact quantities required for the meal.

Eggs: Eggs should not be kept in the refrigerator. Keep them in a cool, dark cupboard for up to two weeks, if they were fresh when bought. Whole yolks can be covered with water and will keep for two or three days, and egg whites will last up to four days if stored in an airtight container.

STORING HERBS AND SPICES

A basic spice rack of ground spices (cinnamon, cloves, paprika, etc.) is a good investment however many people you have to cook for. But certain spices, like nutmeg, are best bought whole and grated as required – and that applies especially to pepper, which rapidly loses its fragrance and aroma unless bought as whole peppercorns and ground from a pepper mill.

Herbs should be bought in small quantities if they are dried, since they lose flavour very quickly. If you grow your own, and it is an undeniable asset to your cooking if you do, you can deep freeze some of your crop. A window box of mint, parsley and chives is easy to take care of, so don't worry if you have no garden of your own.

SUPER STANDBYS

Every clever cook has at least two 'stand-by' foods in her repertoire, and the two-person cook is no exception. Pancakes (crêpes) are a wonderful basic food, and act as an incredibly versatile background to all sorts of flavours and fillings. They can easily be made in advance, and rolled or folded with both sweet and savoury fillings, to make an impressive main course or a mouth-watering dessert.

Unfortunately, cake making on a large scale is not a practical proposition for two. Meringues are an ideal answer – they fall somewhere between a dessert and a cake, and satisfy that need for something sweet to taste. Once made, they can be stored in an airtight tin for up to a few weeks, and there are lots of ways of serving them – plain, sandwiched together, or covered with fruit, chocolate sauce or ice-cream.

EQUIPMENT

There is nothing more off-putting when eating *a deux* to have the meal served on oversized platters and serving dishes. The food seems lost among acres of porcelain, when a little thought could make all the difference. Shop around for small dishes – there is a very popular range of brown earthenware that has delightful containers in various shapes, many with their own lids. Some are meant for other purposes, such as butter and pâté dishes, but you can adapt them to your own uses. You can also buy mini-sized casseroles and pie dishes.

UTENSILS

In order to cook well, you must have the basic tools available, otherwise everything will be twice as hard and take up so much of your time. First and foremost, every cook needs a good set of knives – the carbonated steel ones are best and sharpest – and to begin with you should have at least three of varying length. To keep them sharp, use a butcher's steel or a sharpening stone.

Next on the list is a palette knife, a slotted spoon, a spatula, a long-handled spoon for basting, and of course a set of wooden spoons. For whisking egg whites, nothing does the job better than a balloon whisk, and for other whisking chores a rotary whisk or an electric hand whisk are ideal.

A chopping board is important, otherwise you ruin both your knives and your kitchen surfaces. Every kitchen should have a lemon squeezer, a four-sided grater, a strainer and a colander for draining vegetables (try to avoid the plastic variety). Other important items are a set of scales, or a set of measuring spoons or jugs. Obviously you need a graded set of saucepans, preferably with well fitting lids, and a good set of baking dishes. However, if you are fortunate enough to have all these already, then the one indispensable item in the kitchen has to be a blender.

TECHNIQUES

Several techniques and the use of some ingredients are mentioned throughout this book, and these need explanation.

Deep-frying: This can be done in animal fat (beef suet is best), but vegetable oils are more convenient for most people, and give good, light, crisp results. Use a large, deep pan and fill it one-third full of oil. The oil should be heated over moderate heat to the temperature required. If you have a deep-fat thermometer, this will give a more accurate temperature reading, but a cube of stale bread dropped into the hot oil can be used instead. Generally speaking, raw foods are deep-fried at 180°C/350°F, or when the bread turns light brown in 55 seconds, and cooked foods at 190°C/375°F, or 40 seconds for the bread test. After frying, leave the oil to become completely cold, then strain back into its container.

Blanching: Tomatoes and almonds are just two of the foods which often require blanching. This simply means soaking in boiling water for a few minutes to make the skins easier to remove. Sometimes vegetables are blanched, not to remove the skins, but to partially cook them and so make them more digestible. Green or red peppers used in salads are sometimes blanched for this reason.

Dégorging: Aubergines (eggplants) contain a very high proportion of water. Before cooking them, it is necessary to remove as much water as possible, or the aubergine (eggplant) will absorb too much oil during cooking, making it unpleasantly soggy. Slice the aubergines (eggplants) and place in a colander. Sprinkle with plenty of salt and leave for 30 minutes. Water will collect on the surface and drain away. Rinse the salt off under cold running water and pat dry with absorbent kitchen paper.

Clarifying: Butter burns very quickly when heated, so it is often clarified to stop this happening. To make clarified butter, melt the butter over low heat without allowing it to colour. Skim off any scum as it rises to the surface. Strain through a small strainer, lined with cheesecloth, into a small bowl with a lip. Let the butter settle, then pour into a second bowl, thus leaving the impurities which burn behind.

INGREDIENTS

Seasoned flour: Where seasoned flour is mentioned in the ingredients, for example, to coat meat prior to frying, use the same amount of flour as stated for the seasoned flour, then mix in salt and pepper to taste. For example, for 25 g/1 oz (¼ cup) seasoned flour, use 25 g/1 oz (¼ cup) plain (all-purpose) flour. Finely chopped herbs or ground spices of your choice may also be added.

Herbs and seasonings: Parsley is the most easily obtainable of all herbs, so always try to use it fresh. Quantities given in these recipes are for fresh, finely chopped parsley; if you do use dried, remember to halve the stated quantity for fresh. This goes for all herbs.

Salt and pepper is such a matter of taste, that amounts are not generally given. Black peppercorns, crushed or ground in a pepper mill, give more flavour than ready-ground black pepper. White pepper, milder in flavour than black, is sometimes specified when the appearance of a pale sauce or soup would be spoilt by specks of black pepper.

Flour: Flour is plain (all-purpose) in these recipes, unless otherwise stated.

BASIC RECIPES

SAVOURY PANCAKE (CRÊPE) BATTER

The batter will make 6-8 pancakes (crêpes).

Metric/U.K.		U.S.
75g/3oz	Flour	¾ cup
	Salt	
¾ tsp	Baking powder	¾ tsp
½	Small egg, beaten	½
100ml/4floz	Milk	½ cup
½ Tbsp	Butter, melted	½ Tbsp
1 Tbsp	Vegetable oil	1 Tbsp

Sift flour, salt and baking powder into a mixing bowl. Beat the egg, milk and melted butter together until light and frothy.

Gradually stir the flour mixture into the eggs with a wooden spoon, and beat until batter is smooth.

Brush a heavy-based frying-pan with a little of the oil and heat over moderate heat. Drop 2 to 3 tablespoons of batter on to the pan. Cook for 1 minute. Turn pancake (crêpe) and cook for 1 minute on the other side. Keep hot while you cook the remaining pancakes (crêpes), greasing the pan each time.

Sweet pancake (crêpe) batter.

Sift in ½ Tbsp caster (superfine) sugar with the flour.

MAYONNAISE

This recipe will make about 300ml/½ pint (1¼ cups)

Metric/U.K.		U.S.
2	Large egg yolks	2
½ tsp	French mustard	½ tsp
	Salt	
	White wine vinegar or	
1 Tbsp	lemon juice	1 Tbsp
300ml/½ pint	Olive oil	1¼ cups
1½ Tbsp	Boiling water (optional)	1½ Tbsp

Place egg yolks in a large, warmed mixing bowl and stand bowl on a damp cloth (this holds the bowl firm whilst beating). Beat egg yolks with a wire whisk for 2 minutes until thick and pale. Add mustard, salt and vinegar or lemon juice and beat for 30 seconds.

Add 1 drop of oil and beat in thoroughly. Beat in half the oil, drop by drop. Do not add more than 1 drop at a time or the mixture will curdle. When the mixture is thick, beat in remaining oil, in a slow, steady trickle. The finished mayonnaise should hold its shape and drop heavily from the whisk. Beat in the water, or alternatively more lemon juice or vinegar to thin.

FRENCH DRESSING

This basic French dressing will be enough for a small salad, and makes 50ml/2floz (¼ cup).

Metric/U.K.		U.S.
1 Tbsp	Wine vinegar	1 Tbsp
	Salt and black pepper	
3 Tbsp	Olive oil	3 Tbsp

Measure wine vinegar into a small bowl. Add salt and pepper and stir to dissolve salt. Pour on oil and beat vigorously to mix.

Alternatively, place all the ingredients in a screw top jar and shake briskly.

WHITE SAUCE

This recipe makes 300ml/½ pint (1¼ cups)

Metric/U.K.		U.S.
25g/1oz	Butter	2 Tbsp
25g/1oz	Flour	¼ cup
300ml/½ pint	Milk	1¼ cups
	Salt and white pepper	

Melt the butter over low heat in a small saucepan. Remove pan from heat and stir in flour. Return to the heat and cook for 1 minute, stirring gently. Off the heat gradually stir in the milk.

When all the milk has been incorporated, bring to the boil, season and simmer over low heat for 3 minutes, stirring from time to time.

CHEESE SAUCE

Stir 75g/3oz ($\frac{3}{4}$ cup) grated Cheddar cheese into the sauce just before serving. The heat of the sauce will melt the cheese.

BÉCHAMEL SAUCE

Chop half a small onion, half a small carrot and half a celery stalk. Pour 300ml/$\frac{1}{2}$ pint ($1\frac{1}{4}$ cups) milk into a small pan and add vegetables and a bay leaf. Bring slowly to simmering point, cover then remove from heat. Set aside to infuse for 30 minutes. Strain milk and discard contents of strainer. Use the flavoured milk to make the white sauce.

SHORTCRUST PASTRY

This will make 175g/6oz of pastry.

Metric/U.K.		U.S.
100g/4oz	Flour	1 cup
$\frac{1}{4}$ tsp	Salt	$\frac{1}{4}$ tsp
25g/1oz	Butter or margarine	2 Tbsp
25g/1oz	Lard or cooking fat	2 Tbsp
4 tsp	Cold water	4 tsp

Sift the flour and salt into a mixing bowl. Add fats and cut into small pieces with a knife. Rub fat into flour until mixture resembles breadcrumbs.

Sprinkle over 1 teaspoon water and stir into mixture. Continue adding water, 1 teaspoon at a time, until dough is moist enough to stick together. Add more cold water if necessary.

Draw dough into a ball, and knead lightly on a floured surface. Wrap dough in greaseproof (waxed) paper and chill in the refrigerator for 30 minutes before using.

MAÎTRE D'HÔTEL BUTTER

This recipe will make about 4 pats.

Metric/U.K.		U.S.
50g/2oz	Butter (unsalted if possible), softened	$\frac{1}{4}$ cup
$1\frac{1}{2}$ Tbsp	Chopped parsley	$1\frac{1}{2}$ Tbsp
1 tsp	Lemon juice	1 tsp
	Salt and black pepper	

Place the butter in a small bowl. Add parsley and beat with a wooden spoon until parsley is evenly distributed. Beat in lemon juice, salt and pepper.

Turn butter on to greaseproof (waxed) paper and pat into a roll. Wet your hands and shape into a smooth roll. Wrap in greaseproof (waxed) paper and chill in the refrigerator for 3 hours.

Cut into 6mm/$\frac{1}{4}$ inch thick slices and serve.

VANILLA ICE-CREAM

This will make 600ml/1 pint ($2\frac{1}{2}$ cups)
This ice-cream can easily be made in the frozen food storage compartment of your refrigerator, if you don't have a freezer.

Metric/U.K.		U.S.
600ml/1 pint	Milk	$2\frac{1}{2}$ cups
	Vanilla pod, broken in	
1	half	1
1	Egg yolk	1
	Custard powder or	
1 Tbsp	cornflour (cornstarch)	1 Tbsp
3 Tbsp	Sugar	3 Tbsp
	Gelatine dissolved in	
$1\frac{1}{2}$ tsp	2 Tbsp water	$1\frac{1}{2}$ tsp
1	Egg white, stiffly beaten	1

Set the refrigerator to its coldest setting. Scald the milk with the vanilla pod, remove from heat, cover and set aside to infuse for 20 minutes.

In a mixing bowl, beat egg yolk, custard powder or cornflour (cornstarch), sugar and 2 tablespoons of scalded milk together. Strain remaining milk on to egg yolk mixture, stirring constantly. Pour back into saucepan and cook over low heat for 5 minutes, stirring constantly.

Off the heat, stir in dissolved gelatine. Pour custard into a bowl and set aside to cool. When cold, cover and chill in the freezer or refrigerator for 1 hour.

Pour custard into a freezing tray and freeze for 30 minutes in the freezer or frozen food storage compartment of the refrigerator. Spoon mixture into a chilled bowl and beat well. Fold beaten egg white into custard. Return to freezing tray and freeze for a further 1 hour.

Spoon mixture into the chilled bowl and beat again. Return to its freezing tray and freeze for another hour. The ice-cream is now ready to serve.

APPETIZERS

ANCHOYADE À LA NICOISE

Metric/U.K.		U.S.
	Canned anchovies,	
50g/2oz	drained	2oz
4 tsp	Olive oil	4 tsp
½ tsp	Wine vinegar	½ tsp
	Black pepper	
2	Small onions, chopped	2
2 Tbsp	Chopped parsley	2 Tbsp
	Slices brown bread	
4	toasted on one side	4
2	Tomatoes, sliced	2
2 Tbsp	Fresh breadcrumbs	2 Tbsp
1	Garlic clove, crushed	1

Pound the anchovies in a mortar with a pestle to a paste. Add 3 teaspoons of oil, vinegar and pepper and mix well. Add the onions, parsley (less 1 teaspoon), and spread on the untoasted side of the bread. Place the tomatoes on top. Mix the breadcrumbs, garlic, remaining parsley and remaining oil together and sprinkle on top. Brown under a hot grill (broiler).

WHITEBAIT

Metric/U.K.		U.S.
¼kg/½lb	Whitebait, fresh	½lb
	Seasoned flour	
	Oil for deep-frying	
	Salt	
	Cayenne pepper	
	Parsley sprigs	
1	Lemon, cut into wedges	1

Rinse the whitebait thoroughly, drain well and dry on absorbent kitchen paper. Toss the fish gently in seasoned flour, making sure each one is evenly coated. Shake off any surplus flour.

Heat a deep pan one-third full of oil to 180°C/350°F. Put the whitebait in a deep-frying basket, a few at a time, and lower into the oil. Fry for 2 to 3 minutes until crisp. Shake the basket from time to time to keep fish separate.

Drain the fish on absorbent kitchen paper and fry the remaining fish.

Serve the whitebait sprinkled with salt and cayenne pepper and garnished with parsley sprigs and lemon wedges.

DEVILS ON HORSEBACK

Originally served as a savoury in between courses, when long, large meals were commonplace.

Metric/U.K.		U.S.
75ml/3floz	Water or dry red wine	⅓ cup
	Large canned prunes,	
6	drained	6

Bottom: *Devils on Horseback;* Opposite page: *Deep-fried Whitebait*

	Canned anchovy fillets,	
6	drained	6
6	Blanched almonds	6
	Bacon slices, rinds removed and cut in half	
3	crosswise	3
	Small triangles hot	
6	buttered toast	6
	Watercress sprigs	

Bring the water or wine to the boil in a small saucepan over high heat. Add prunes and set aside to soak for 40 minutes.

Place pan over moderate heat and simmer prunes until almost all of the liquid has been absorbed. Cool, then stone the prunes.

Preheat the oven to 220°C/425°F (gas mark 7). Wrap an anchovy fillet around each almond and insert into prunes. Wrap a bacon piece around each prune and secure with a wooden cocktail stick (toothpick). Place prunes on a baking sheet and roast for 10 minutes. Remove prunes from oven and place each one on a toast triangle. Arrange on a warmed plate and garnish with watercress.

Steamed asparagus with butter sauce

ASPARAGUS

Always steam this delicate vegetable as boiling will make it limp and unappetizing. If you don't have a steamer basket, improvise by laying the bundles in between 2 large heat-proof plates set over a pan of simmering water. Asparagus will take longer to cook by this method, so allow an extra 10 minutes. Special asparagus pans are available but these are expensive and not worth buying unless you grow or have access to a large amount of asparagus. Serve with melted butter or any of the sauces given for Artichokes (see page 21).

Metric/U.K.		U.S.
16	Asparagus stalks	16

Wash the asparagus carefully to remove any grit. Trim off woody ends and scrape the stems with a sharp knife to remove scaly leaf points. Tie into 2 equal bundles (8 stalks each); keeping the bases of the stems level, tie with string just below tips and

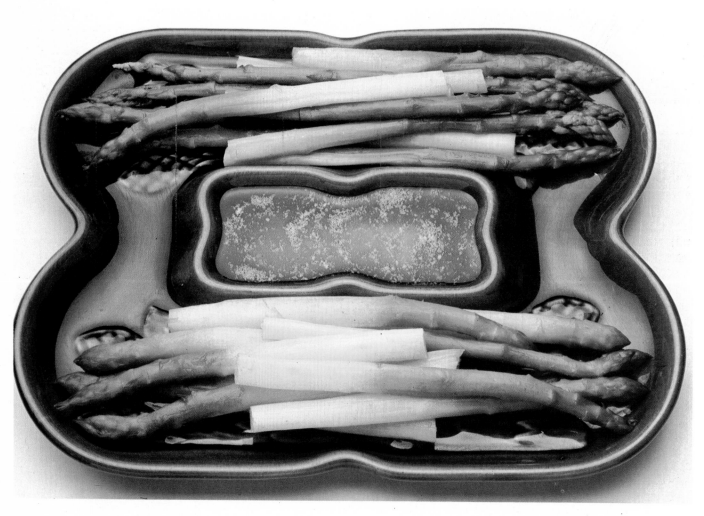

Grapefruit and Avocado Salad

again further down stems. Pour a little water into a large pan fitted with a tight fitting lid. Position a steamer basket, fully opened, into the pan. The water should not come through the holes in the basket. Bring the water to the boil. Lay the bundles out flat in the basket. Cover and return to the boil. Reduce the heat to very low and steam for 10 to 15 minutes, depending on size. Check water level from time to time and top up with boiling water if necessary.

Carefully lift the bundles out of the basket and arrange in a serving dish. Remove string and serve. Asparagus may be eaten in the fingers and dipping into a sauce of your choice.

GRAPEFRUIT AND AVOCADO SALAD

Metric/U.K.		U.S.
	Large, ripe avocado pear,	
	halved and stoned	
1	(pitted)	1
1 tsp	Lemon juice	1 tsp
	Small grapefruit, peeled,	
	pith removed and	
1	chopped	1
	Chicory (French or	
	Belgian endive), trimmed	
½ head	and chopped	½ head
1 tsp	Sugar	1 tsp
	French dressing (see	
1½ Tbsp	page 12)	1½ Tbsp

Using a teaspoon, scoop out the avocado flesh and place it in a mixing bowl. Reserve shells.

Add ½ teaspoon of the lemon juice, the grapefruit, chicory (endive) and sugar and, using a fork, mash together until smooth.

Stir in French dressing. Spoon the mixture into the avocado shells and sprinkle over remaining lemon juice. Chill in the refrigerator for about 30 minutes before serving.

17

Hot Spiced Grapefruit

EGG FOO YUNG

Always use fresh bean sprouts for the best flavour and crunchy texture.

Metric/U.K.		U.S.
4	Eggs	4
1 Tbsp	Soy sauce	1 Tbsp
	Salt and black pepper	
25g/1oz	Butter	2 Tbsp
	Small onions, finely	
1	chopped	1
100g/¼lb	Bean sprouts washed	2 cups
	Cooked ham, cut into	
50g/2oz	thin strips	2oz

Beat the eggs, soy sauce, salt and pepper together with a wire whisk until light and fluffy. Melt the butter in a frying-pan and fry the onion, bean sprouts and ham for 4 to 5 minutes, stirring from time to time. Pour the beaten egg mixture into the pan, stir with a fork and leave to set.

When the bottom of the omelette is set, remove pan from heat and place under a hot grill (broiler). Grill (broil) until the top is set and lightly browned. Cut into wedges and serve at once.

HOT SPICED GRAPEFRUIT

Metric/U.K.		U.S.
2 Tbsp	Soft (light) brown sugar	2 Tbsp
a pinch	Ground allspice	a pinch
¼ tsp	Ground cinnamon	¼ tsp
2 tsp	Butter, softened	2 tsp
2 tsp	Dark rum	2 tsp
	Large grapefruit, halved	
1	and flesh loosened	1
2	Mint sprigs	2

Combine the sugar, allspice and cinnamon in a small bowl. Add the butter and rum. Cream the mixture with a wooden spoon until it forms a smooth paste. Divide the mixture and spread over each grapefruit half. Cook under a hot grill (broiler) for 6 to 8 minutes or until sugar mixture has melted and is bubbling. Serve at once, garnished with mint.

JAPANESE SARDINES

Don't be tempted to use canned sardines, as the strong oil or sauce in which they are canned will mask the delicate flavour of the marinade.

Metric/U.K.		U.S.
50ml/2floz	Soy sauce	¼ cup
2 Tbsp	Wine vinegar	2 Tbsp
1 Tbsp	Lemon juice	1 Tbsp
	Fresh root ginger, peeled	
1cm/½in piece	and chopped	½in piece
1	Garlic clove, crushed	1
	Fresh sardines, washed	
	thoroughly in cold water	
¼kg/½lb	and dried	½ lb
1 Tbsp	Olive oil	1 Tbsp

Combine the soy sauce, vinegar, lemon juice, ginger and garlic. Arrange the sardines in a shallow heatproof dish and pour mixture over. Marinate in a cool place for 2 hours.

Remove sardines from marinade and dry fish on absorbent kitchen paper. Discard marinade. Line a grill (broiler) pan with foil and brush with half the oil. Place sardines on foil and brush them with remaining oil. Cook under moderately high grill (broiler) for 3 to 5 minutes, depending on size, turning once to cook both sides. Serve at once.

ARTICHOKES

Globe artichokes are fun to eat and delicious. The leaves are pulled away, dipped in melted butter or sauce, then the fleshy leaf base is pulled between your teeth. When all the outer leaves have been eaten, use a knife and fork to

Japanese sardines

cut the artichoke heart into chunks; this is considered to be the best part. Provide small dishes of melted butter (if you are serving them hot), or French dressing or mayonnaise (see Basic Recipes) if they are cold, and a large plate for discarded leaves. Plenty of napkins and finger bowls (filled with warm water and a slice of lemon) are also a good idea as it can be a messy business!

It is probably easier to remove the chokes before cooking, as the artichokes will be difficult to handle when hot.

Metric/U.K.		U.S.
2	Globe artichokes	2
½	Lemon	½
	Water	
	Salt	

Cut the stalks off the artichokes and pull off any bruised or tough outer leaves. Slice off the top quarter of the artichoke. With kitchen scissors, trim the tips of the leaves. Wash well under cold running water. Rub the cut edges of the artichoke with the lemon to prevent discoloration.

To remove chokes before cooking, gently spread the top leaves apart and pull out prickly leaves surrounding the hairy choke. Scrape out the choke with a teaspoon. Squeeze a little lemon juice into the centre and press leaves back together again.

Heat a large saucepan two-thirds full of water to boiling point. Add salt. Drop the artichokes in, base down, and bring back to the boil. Reduce heat to moderate and cook, uncovered, for 15 minutes, turning the artichokes from time to time. If the chokes have not been removed, cook for 30 minutes. The artichokes are cooked when the base is tender when pierced with a sharp knife and the leaves pull out easily. Drain upside down in a colander, and remove choke with a teaspoon, if not removed before cooking.

TARAMASALATA

Tarama is the dried, pressed roe of the grey mullet, traditionally used to make this Greek hors d'oeuvre. Cod's roe is a good substitute.

Metric/U.K.		U.S.
175g/6oz	Tarama or smoked cod's roe, skinned	6oz

Top: Taramasalata, with the traditional accompaniment of pita
Opposite page: Artichokes being boiled

Beat the pepper into the taramasalata and arrange on 2 small plates. Surround with cucumber and tomato slices and top each portion with an olive. Serve at once.

ROES ON TOAST

Metric/U.K.		U.S.
¼ tsp	Dry mustard	¼ tsp
1 Tbsp	Seasoned flour	1 Tbsp
¼kg/½lb	Soft herring roes	½lb
15g/½oz	Butter	1 Tbsp
2 slices	Hot buttered toast	2 slices
2 tsp	Chopped parsley	2 tsp
1	Lemon, cut into wedges	1

Mix the dry mustard with the seasoned flour. Dip each roe in the flour to coat completely and shake off any excess.

Melt the butter and cook the roes for 8 to 10 minutes, turning once, until lightly browned and tender.

Place toast on 2 serving plates and spoon roes on top of toast. Sprinkle with parsley and garnish with lemon wedges. Serve at once.

TOMATO CHEESE SAVOURY

Metric/U.K.		U.S.
15g/½oz	Butter	1 Tbsp
½	Small onion, chopped	½
2	Tomatoes, blanched, peeled and sliced	2
25g/1oz	Grated Parmesan cheese	¼ cup
	Salt	
¼ tsp	Paprika	¼ tsp
1	Egg, well beaten	1
2 slices	Hot buttered toast	2 slices
GARNISH		
1	Small tomato, blanched, peeled, and cut into strips	1

Melt the butter and fry the onion and tomatoes for 4 minutes until soft. Add cheese, salt and paprika and stir in the egg. Continue cooking, stirring from time to time for 2 to 3 minutes or until mixture has thickened.

Place toast on 2 serving plates and carefully pile the egg mixture on to the toast. Garnish with tomato strips and serve at once.

Roes on Toast

	Slices white bread, crusts removed and soaked in milk for 15	
2	minutes	2
2	Garlic cloves, crushed	2
100ml/4floz	Olive oil	½ cup
4 tsp	Lemon juice	4 tsp
	Freshly ground black pepper	
GARNISH		
	Cucumber slices	
	Tomato slices	
2	Black olives	2

Pound the cod's roes in a mortar with a pestle until it is smooth. Squeeze as much moisture out of the bread as possible and add the bread to the bowl with the garlic. Pound until smooth.

Add the oil, a few drops at a time, pounding constantly and adding a little of the lemon juice from time to time. Continue pounding until the mixture forms a pale pink, soft, smooth paste. Alternatively blend in an electric blender.

SHRIMP AVOCADO COCKTAIL

Metric/U.K.		U.S.
I	Large avocado	I
I tsp	Lemon juice	I tsp
2 Tbsp	Mayonnaise (see page 12)	2 Tbsp
2 tsp	Double (heavy) cream	2 tsp
small	Salt and black pepper	small
pinch	Cayenne pepper	pinch
½ tsp	Mild curry powder	½ tsp
I	Canned pineapple ring, drained and finely chopped	I
50g/2oz	Shrimps, shelled (peeled)	2 oz

Cut the avocado in half lengthways. Remove and discard the stones (pits) and place each half in a serving dish. Set aside.

Combine the lemon juice, mayonnaise, cream, salt and pepper, cayenne pepper and curry powder. Beat until well blended. Stir in the pineapple and shrimps. Spoon the mixture into the avocado halves and serve at once.

LIVER SAUSAGE AND EGG SPREAD

Covered, this will keep for up to 2 days in the refrigerator.

Metric/U.K.		U.S.
2	Eggs, hard-boiled (hardcooked) and finely chopped	2
100g/¼lb	Liver sausage	¼lb
¼ tsp	Dried thyme	¼ tsp
¼ tsp	Dried sage	¼ tsp
	Salt and pepper	

Combine all the ingredients and mash to a smooth paste. Alternatively, blend in an electric blender. Serve at once, or cover with foil and chill in the refrigerator until required.

Shrimp Avocado Cocktail

STUFFED TOMATOES

To serve cold, allow the tomatoes to cool in the dish, then chill in the refrigerator for at least 1 hour before serving.

Metric/U.K.		U.S.
4	Large firm tomatoes	4
3 Tbsp	Olive oil	3 Tbsp
1	Small onion, finely chopped	1
½	Garlic clove, crushed	½
50g/2oz	Fresh breadcrumbs	1 cup
4	Canned anchovy fillets, drained and chopped	4
8	Black olives, stoned (pitted) and chopped	8
1 Tbsp	Chopped parsley	1 Tbsp
½ tsp	Dried oregano	½ tsp
4 tsp	Grated Parmesan cheese	4 tsp
2 tsp	Butter, cut into 4 pieces	2 tsp

Preheat oven to 180°C/350°F (gas mark 4).

Cut off tops of tomatoes and discard tops. Scoop out the seeds with a teaspoon, taking care not to pierce the skin. Discard seeds and set tomatoes aside.

Heat the oil over moderate heat in a large frying-pan. Add onion and garlic and fry for 5 minutes until soft. Remove pan from heat and stir in breadcrumbs, anchovies, olives, parsley and oregano. Fill tomatoes with breadcrumb mixture. Place tomatoes in an ovenproof dish, large enough to take them in one layer. Sprinkle over Parmesan and top each with a piece of butter. Bake for 20 to 25 minutes or until lightly browned. Serve immediately.

KIPPER PÂTÉ

If you do not possess an electric blender, mash the kipper fillets and butter first and gradually beat in the remaining ingredients.

Metric/U.K.		U.S.
175g/6oz	Boned kipper fillets, poached, skinned and flaked	6oz
15g/½oz	Butter, melted	1 Tbsp
1 tsp	Sweet sherry (optional)	1 tsp
2 Tbsp	Double (heavy) cream	2 Tbsp
½ tsp	Worcestershire sauce	½ tsp

Stuffed Tomatoes

Baked Avocado

Metric/U.K.		U.S.
15g/½oz	Black pepper Clarified butter, melted (see page 11)	1 Tbsp

Put the kippers, melted butter, sherry (if you are using it), cream, Worcestershire sauce and pepper to taste in an electric blender. Blend until smooth.

Spoon pâté into a small dish and smooth over the top. Pour over the clarified butter and chill in the refrigerator for at least 2 hours before serving.

BAKED AVOCADO

Metric/U.K.		U.S.
3	Slices white bread	3
25g/1oz	Salami, skinned and diced	1oz
2	Small eggs, hard-boiled (hard-cooked) and chopped	2
25g/1oz	Butter	2 Tbsp
¼ tsp	Dry mustard	¼ tsp
½ tsp	Curry powder	½ tsp
	Salt and black pepper	
3 Tbsp	Milk	3 Tbsp
1	Avocado	1
	Lemon juice	
1	Lemon, cut into wedges	1

Grate bread into crumbs. Reserve three-quarters of crumbs for stuffing and toast the remainder.

Put reserved breadcrumbs, salami and eggs into a mixing bowl. Melt half the butter and pour into bowl. Add mustard, curry powder, salt, pepper and milk. Mix to blend well. Cover the bowl and set aside. Preheat oven to 190°C/375°F (gas mark 5).

Halve and stone (pit) the avocado. Brush cut surfaces with lemon juice to prevent discoloration. Grease a baking dish and put avocado halves into it. Fill with stuffing and press down with back of spoon. Sprinkle with toasted breadcrumbs and dot with remaining butter. Bake for 20 to 25 minutes or until tops are well browned. Serve at once with lemon wedges.

OEUFS SUR LA PLAT

The secret of this French way of cooking eggs is to cover the dish. This traps a small amount of steam which lightly cooks the surface of the eggs.

Metric/U.K.		U.S.
6 tsp	Butter	6 tsp
4	Eggs	4
	Salt and black pepper	

Bacon Rolls

Divide 4 tsp of the butter between 2 individual flameproof dishes. Melt over moderate heat (using 2 hot plates or rings). Break 2 eggs into each dish.

Cover the dishes and cook over moderate heat for 4 to 5 minutes. Season the whites with salt and pepper and dot the remaining butter over the egg yolks. Serve at once.

LEEKS VINAIGRETTE

A substantial first course. For added flavour, substitute 1 tablespoon of hot bacon fat for 1 tablespoon of the olive oil. If you do this, however, serve the dish soon after cooking as congealed bacon fat is unappetizing to say the least!

Metric/U.K.		U.S.
3	Lean bacon slices, grilled (broiled) until crisp and chopped	3
350g/¾lb	Leeks, cooked and chopped	¾lb
2	Eggs, hard-boiled (hardcooked) and sliced	2
2 tsp	Chopped parsley	2 tsp

DRESSING

½	Garlic clove, crushed	½
	Salt and pepper	
pinch	Dried oregano	pinch
1 Tbsp	Tarragon vinegar	1 Tbsp
3 Tbsp	Olive oil	3 Tbsp

Combine the bacon, leeks and eggs in a medium-sized salad bowl, and set aside.

Place all the dressing ingredients in a screw top jar. Shake briskly, pour over the leek mixture and toss well. Sprinkle with parsley and serve at once.

BACON ROLLS

Metric/U.K.		U.S.
25g/1oz	Butter	2 Tbsp
½	Small onion, coarsely chopped	½
50g/2oz	Mushrooms, wiped clean and coarsely chopped	½ cup
	Black pepper	
½ tsp	Lemon juice	½ tsp
	Fresh breadcrumbs soaked in 2 tsp chicken	

8g/¼oz	stock	⅛ cup
½ tsp	Chopped parsley	½ tsp
4	Lean bacon slices, rinds removed	4

In a small saucepan, melt the butter over low heat. Reserve 1 teaspoon. Add onion and mushrooms and cook for 3 minutes or until mushrooms are soft. Remove from heat and transfer onion and mushrooms to a mixing bowl. Add pepper, lemon juice, breadcrumb mixture and parsley. Mash to a paste.

Lay bacon slices out flat and spread each slice with paste. Roll up and thread on to skewers. Place skewers on grill (broiler) rack and brush bacon rolls with reserved melted butter. Grill (broil) under high heat, turning frequently, for 6 to 8 minutes, or until crisp. Remove the skewers from the heat. Serve at once.

MELON AND HAM

Prosciutto is Italian, raw, air-cured ham with a fine, delicate flavour which complements melon beautifully. Substitute any cooked ham if prosciutto is unavailable.

Metric/U.K.		U.S.
2 slices	Cantaloup melon, seeded	2 slices
50g/2oz	Prosciutto, thinly sliced and cut into 8 strips	2oz

Cut the flesh from the skin of the melon slices. Return the flesh to the skin to form its original shape. Make 4 'V' shapes at equal distances along the length of each melon slice.

Roll up each strip of prosciutto neatly. Place a roll in each cut and serve at once.

CARROT AND CREAM CHEESE PÂTÉ

Metric/U.K.		U.S.
½kg/1lb	Carrots, chopped	1lb
175g/6oz	Cream cheese	¾ cup
1 tsp	Chopped parsley	1 tsp
	Salt and black pepper	
1 tsp	Chopped fresh chives	1 tsp
GARNISH		
	Watercress sprigs	
	Cucumber slices	

Melon and Ham

Cook the carrots in boiling salted water for 7 minutes. Drain and mash to give a rough purée. Allow to become cold, then beat in the cheese. Add parsley, salt, pepper and chives and mix until well blended.

Line a small loaf tin with greaseproof (wax) paper. Press mixture firmly into tin and level the top with a knife. Cover with foil and chill in the refrigerator for 3 hours.

Run a knife between pâté and tin to loosen. Place a serving plate on top and invert. Garnish with watercress springs and cucumber slices. Serve at once.

HERB-STUFFED EGGS

Metric/U.K.		U.S.
	Eggs, hard-boiled	
2	(hardcooked)	2
1 Tbsp	Single (light) cream	1 Tbsp
1 tsp	Fresh chopped chives	1 tsp
1 tsp	Fresh chopped dill	1 tsp
1 tsp	Chopped parsley	1 tsp
	Salt and pepper	
	Watercress	

Halve the eggs lengthways. Remove yolks

and rub yolks through a strainer. Add cream, herbs, salt and pepper and beat thoroughly to mix.

Use a teaspoon to mound the mixture into the egg whites, or pipe the stuffing using a forcing bag and star nozzle. Arrange eggs in a small dish on a bed of watercress.

MACKEREL AND ONION SALAD

Metric/U.K.		U.S.
	Canned mackerel,	
200g/7oz	drained and flaked	7oz
	Small onion, coarsely	
1	chopped	1
	Salt and pepper	
1 Tbsp	Tomato purée (paste)	1 Tbsp
1 Tbsp	Lemon juice	1 Tbsp
	Crisp lettuce separated	
$\frac{1}{2}$	into leaves	$\frac{1}{2}$
GARNISH		
	Tomato slices	
	Cucumber slices	
	Chopped parsley	

Combine the mackerel, onion, salt, pepper,

Carrot and Cream Cheese Pâté, with a garnish of cucumbers and watercress

tomato purée (paste) and lemon juice and mash together until well blended.

Line a serving plate with the lettuce leaves. Spoon mackerel mixture on to lettuce and arrange tomato and cucumber slices alternately around the edge of the plate. Sprinkle with parsley and chill in the refrigerator for 30 minutes before serving.

GRILLED SPRATS

It is a pity that sprats are a seasonal fish as they are nutritious, cheap and a delight to eat, especially when cooked in this way, on their own little 'washing lines'.

Metric/U.K.		U.S.
350g/¾lb	Sprats	¾lb
2 Tbsp	Vegetable oil	2 Tbsp
	Salt and black pepper	
1	Lemon, cut into wedges	1

Wash the sprats and dry with absorbent kitchen paper. Place sprats in a shallow dish, add oil, salt and pepper and stir gently to coat each fish with oil and seasoning.

Thread the sprats through the heads on 2 skewers, spacing them out so that each fish will lie flat on the grill (broiler) rack without overlapping. Place skewers on rack in pan and grill (broil) close to high heat until crisp and golden. Turn each skewer carefully and cook for a further 2 to 3 minutes.

Ease sprats off skewers with a fork and serve at once with lemon wedges.

TUNA PUFFS

Metric/U.K.		U.S.
200g/7oz	Canned tuna fish, drained and flaked	7oz
2	Spring onions (scallions), trimmed and finely chopped	2
25g/1oz	Flour	¼ cup
2	Eggs, separated	2
	Salt and pepper	
¼ tsp	Cayenne pepper	¼ tsp
	Oil for deep-frying	

Place tuna fish and spring onions (scallions) in a mixing bowl. Add flour, egg yolks, salt, pepper and cayenne and beat well to mix.

Mackerel and Onion Salad

Sausage and Pepper Rolls

Beat the egg whites until stiff. Using a large metal spoon, fold whites into tuna fish mixture.

Heat a deep pan one-third full of oil to 180°C/350°F. Carefully drop tablespoons of the mixture in to the oil, about 5 or 6 at a time, and fry for 3 to 4 minutes or until golden brown and crisp. Drain on absorbent kitchen paper and keep hot while you fry the remaining mixture. Serve at once.

a further 15 minutes or until peppers are tender. Place peppers in a warmed dish, sprinkle with salt and basil and keep hot.

Heat the oil over moderate heat. Remove from heat. Place the bread rolls cut sides up, on the grill (broiler) rack. Top each with a slice of sausage and a pepper half. Sprinkle over cheese and drip hot oil on top. Grill (broil) for 4 minutes or until topping is golden. Serve at once.

SAUSAGE AND PEPPER ROLLS

Metric/U.K.		U.S.
	Large green peppers, halved, pith removed	
2	and seeded	2
	Salt	
¼ tsp	Dried basil	¼ tsp
1½ tsp	Olive oil	1½ tsp
	Italian bread rolls,	
2	halved	2
4 slices	Mortadella sausage	4 slices
40g/1½oz	Grated Parmesan cheese	½ cup

Arrange halved peppers, skin sides up, on grill (broiler) rack and cook under hot grill (broiler) for 15 minutes. Turn and cook for

JELLIED EGGS

The consommé is chilled before use to make it jell.

Metric/U.K.		U.S.
	Canned anchovy fillets,	
4	drained	4
	Canned concentrated beef or chicken	
100ml/4floz	consommé, well chilled	½ cup
	Eggs, soft-boiled	
2	(soft-cooked)	2
50ml/2floz	Sour cream	¼ cup
1	Lemon, cut into wedges	1

Cut 2 of the anchovy fillets in half and finely chop the remainder. Turn the jellied

consommé into a bowl and chop roughly to break up a little. Put a little of the jelly in 2 serving bowls. Place an egg in each bowl and surround with a few chopped anchovies. Cover the anchovies with a dribble of sour cream, and cover cream with remaining jelly and anchovies. Pour a little sour cream over each egg and top with the halved anchovy fillets arranged in a cross.

Chill in the refrigerator for 30 minutes, before serving garnished with lemon wedges.

SMOKED SALMON WITH SCRAMBLED EGGS

Some fishmongers sell smoked salmon pieces (irregular-shaped off-cuts) very cheaply. Fairly large slices are sometimes included which are ideal for this recipe as they will make it less expensive.

Metric/U.K.		U.S.
1	Small lettuce heart, finely shredded	1
25g/1oz	Butter	2 Tbsp
½	Small green pepper, pith removed, seeded and finely chopped	½
2	Eggs, lightly beaten	2
2 tsp	Fresh chives, chopped	2 tsp
	Salt and black pepper	
a pinch	Grated nutmeg	a pinch
3 Tbsp	Single (light) cream	3 Tbsp
175g/6oz	Smoked salmon, thinly sliced	6oz
⅛ tsp	Paprika	⅛ tsp
1	Lemon, quartered	1

Jellied Eggs

Arrange lettuce on a serving dish and set aside.

Melt the butter in a small saucepan, add the pepper and cook for 5 minutes, stirring frequently. Add eggs, chives, salt and pepper, nutmeg and cream and cook for about 5 minutes, stirring constantly, until the mixture thickens. Transfer mixture to a mixing bowl and set aside to cool completely.

Lay salmon slices out flat. Spread each slice with a little of the egg mixture and roll up. Arrange rolls on the lettuce, sprinkle with paprika and garnish with lemon. Serve at once.

EGGS STUFFED WITH 'CAVIAR'

Lumpfish roe is an exceptionally cheap 'substitute' for caviar at a fraction of the cost.

31

Metric/U.K.		U.S.
	Eggs, hard-boiled	
2	(hardcooked)	2
2 tsp	Lumpfish roe	2 tsp
½ tsp	Lemon juice	½ tsp
small		small
pinch	Cayenne pepper	pinch
	Watercress	

Cut the eggs in half lengthways. Cut a thin slice off the bottom of each half so the eggs will stand firm. Remove the yolks and mash with a fork.

Beat the lumpfish roe, lemon juice and cayenne pepper into the yolks. Spoon the mixture into the whites. Arrange the stuffed eggs on a serving dish and chill in the refrigerator for 30 minutes.

Garnish with watercress before serving.

STUFFED MUSHROOMS

Metric/U.K.		U.S.
	Large mushrooms wiped	
	clean, trimmed and	
4	stalks reserved	4
	Salt and black pepper	
small		small
pinch	Dry mustard	pinch
small		small
pinch	Sugar	pinch
1 Tbsp	Wine vinegar	1 Tbsp
2 Tbsp	Olive oil	2 Tbsp
½ Tbsp	Chopped parsley	½ Tbsp
1	Slice stale white bread	1
	Small eggs, hard-boiled	
2	(hard-cooked)	2
2 tsp	Sour cream	2 tsp
	Parsley sprigs	

Place mushroom caps, gills upwards, in a shallow glass or earthenware dish. Put salt, pepper, mustard and sugar in a screw-top jar. Pour on vinegar and stir with a fork. Add oil, screw the top on tightly and shake. Pour marinade over mushrooms, cover dish and leave for 4 hours, basting from time to time.

Chop reserved mushroom stalks and mix with chopped parsley. Grate bread into crumbs. Halve eggs, rub yolks through a strainer and chop whites finely. Mix mushroom stalks, herbs, breadcrumbs and eggs together. Season to taste.

Transfer mushrooms to a serving plate. Add any marinade not absorbed by the mushrooms to the egg mixture and mix. Stir in sour cream. Mound stuffing in centre of each mushroom and garnish with parsley sprigs.

KIDNEY AND MUSHROOM CROÛTES

Metric/U.K.		U.S.
	Thick slices bread,	
	2cm/¾in thick, crusts	
2	removed	2

Below: *Eggs Stuffed with Caviar;* Bottom: *Stuffed Mushrooms*

1	Small egg	1
5 Tbsp	Milk	5 Tbsp
25g/1oz	Butter	2 Tbsp
2	Lean bacon slices, rinds removed and chopped	2
2	Lambs' kidneys, cleaned prepared and chopped	2
100g/¼lb	Mushrooms, wiped clean and chopped	1 cup
2 tsp	Lemon juice	2 tsp
	Salt and pepper	
2 Tbsp	Vegetable oil	2 Tbsp
2	Hot poached eggs	2

Using a sharp knife, slightly hollow out the centres of the bread slices so that there is a 1 cm ½ inch deep indentation in each one. Whisk the egg and milk in a deep plate, add the bread and leave to soak.

In a frying-pan melt half the butter, add the bacon and fry for 5 minutes. Add kidney and cook for a further 5 minutes, stirring from time to time. Add mushrooms and cook for 3 minutes, stirring constantly. Stir in lemon juice, salt and pepper. Reduce the heat to low and simmer for 2 minutes. Using a slotted spoon, remove mixture from pan and keep hot.

Melt the remaining butter in the pan with the oil. Fry the bread slices for 2 minutes on each side until golden brown and crisp. Drain on absorbent kitchen paper. Arrange on 2 serving plates, hollow sides up, and fill hollows with the kidney mixture. Place poached eggs on top and serve at once.

Kidney and Mushroom Croûtes

SOUPS

TOMATO SOUP

Metric/U.K.		U.S.
1 Tbsp	Butter	1 Tbsp
350g/¾lb	Tomatoes, quartered	¾lb
450ml/¾ pint	Chicken stock	2 cups
1	Small onion, finely chopped	1
1	Bay leaf	1
	Salt and black pepper	
1 Tbsp	Thinly pared orange rind	1 Tbsp
1 tsp	Lemon juice	1 tsp
½ tsp	Sugar	½ tsp

In a large saucepan melt the butter and cook the tomatoes over low heat for 5 minutes, stirring frequently. Increase heat and add stock, onion, bay leaf, salt, pepper and orange rind. Bring to the boil, reduce heat to low, cover and simmer for 40 minutes.

Strain the soup, pressing tomatoes to extract juices. Discard contents of strainer. Rinse out saucepan and return strained soup. Place pan over low heat and stir in lemon juice and sugar. Bring slowly to the boil, stirring frequently. Ladle soup into individual soup bowls and serve at once.

CELERY AND ALMOND SOUP

Metric/U.K.		U.S.
25g/1oz	Butter	2 Tbsp
¼kg/½lb	Celery, chopped	½lb
	Salt and black pepper	
300ml/½ pint	Chicken stock	1¼ cups
1	Parsley sprig	1
300ml/½ pint	Milk	1¼ cups
2 Tbsp	Single (light) cream	2 Tbsp
2 Tbsp	Toasted flaked almonds	2 Tbsp

In a large saucepan melt the butter and

Below: *Tomato Soup*; Opposite page: *Celery and Almond Soup*

cook the celery over low heat for 10 minutes, shaking the pan from time to time. Season with salt and pepper and pour in stock. Add parsley. Bring to the boil, reduce heat to low, cover and simmer for 20 minutes. Add milk.

Strain the soup, pressing celery to extract juices. Discard contents of strainer. Rinse out saucepan and return soup to pan. Reheat gently. Ladle into individual soup bowls and stir a little cream into each. Sprinkle with toasted almonds and serve at once.

YOGHURT SOUP

Metric/U.K.		U.S.
300ml/½ pint	Plain yoghurt	1¼ cups
50ml/2floz	Single (light) cream	¼ cup
50ml/2floz	Water	¼ cup
2 tsp	Lemon juice	2 tsp
½	Cucumber, peeled, finely chopped and degorged	½
1	Small red dessert apple, cored and diced	1
½	Small onion, finely chopped	½
25g/1oz	Seedless raisins, soaked in water for 5 minutes and drained	2 Tbsp
25g/1oz	Shelled pistachio nuts, chopped	¼ cup
	Salt	
¼ tsp	Ground cumin	¼ tsp
¼ tsp	Turmeric	¼ tsp
3	Ice cubes	3
2 tsp	Chopped parsley	2 tsp

In a soup tureen, combine yoghurt, cream, water and lemon juice. Stir in cucumber, apple, onion, raisins and nuts. In a cup, combine salt, cumin and turmeric and stir into yoghurt mixture.

Chill soup in the refrigerator for 30 minutes. Add ice cubes, sprinkle with parsley and serve.

CHICKEN SOUP

Chicken pieces are easily obtainable and are more economical for 2 people than buying a small chicken. You will need about ½ kg/1 lb of chicken to yield 100 g/¼ lb of boned meat.

Metric/U.K.		U.S.
½ Tbsp	Olive oil	½ Tbsp
3	Spring onions (scallions), trimmed and finely chopped	3
2	Lean bacon slices, rinds removed and chopped	2
¼ tsp	Dried tarragon	¼ tsp
100g/¼lb	Raw chicken meat, cut into thin strips	¼lb
2 Tbsp	Dry white wine	2 Tbsp
450ml/¾ pint	Chicken stock	2 cups
1½ Tbsp	Grated Parmesan cheese	1½ Tbsp

In a large saucepan heat the oil over moderate heat. Add spring onions (scallions), bacon and tarragon and fry for 4 minutes. Add chicken and fry for further 6 minutes, stirring from time to time. Add wine and enough stock to cover chicken. Bring to boil, reduce heat to low, cover and simmer for 20 minutes.

Pour remaining stock into pan and bring to the boil, stirring frequently. Ladle soup into individual soup bowls, sprinkle with cheese and serve at once.

SPICY HOT AND SOUR SOUP

Home-made beef stock will make this soup taste even better.

Metric/U.K.		U.S.
450ml/¾ pint	Beef stock	2 cups
1 Tbsp	Soy sauce	1 Tbsp
¼ tsp	Chilli sauce	¼ tsp
	Salt and black pepper	
50g/2oz	Rump steak, cut into thin strips	2oz
50g/2oz	Canned bamboo shoots, drained and chopped	2oz
2	Spring onions (scallions), trimmed and cut in half	2
2	Large mushrooms, wiped clean and sliced	2
1 Tbsp	Dry sherry	1 Tbsp

In a large saucepan bring stock to boil. Add soy sauce, chilli sauce, salt, pepper and steak. Reduce heat to low and simmer uncovered for 5 minutes. Add bamboo shoots, spring onions (scallions) and mushrooms and simmer for a further 4 minutes.

Remove from heat and stir in sherry. Ladle soup into individual soup bowls and serve at once.

SOUR CREAM AND 'CAVIAR' SOUP

A ritzy soup which takes minutes to prepare.

Metric/U.K.		U.S.
	Canned condensed beef	
300ml/½ pint	consommé, chilled	1¼ cups
1½ Tbsp	Sour cream	1½ Tbsp
40g/1½oz	Lumpfish roe	3 Tbsp

Place consommé into a mixing bowl and break up with a fork. Divide consommé between individual soup bowls. Spoon sour cream and lumpfish roe over the consommé and serve at once.

TURNIP SOUP

Metric/U.K.		U.S.
25g/1oz	Butter	2 Tbsp
	Large turnip, peeled	
1	and chopped	1
	Medium-sized potato,	
1	peeled and chopped	1
1	Small onion, chopped	1
2 tsp	Flour	2 tsp
600ml/1 pint	Hot chicken stock	2½ cups
	Salt and black pepper	
1	Bay leaf	1
¼ tsp	Grated nutmeg	¼ tsp
75ml/3floz	Single (light) cream	⅓ cup
	Small carrot, scraped	
1	and grated	1

In a large saucepan melt the butter and fry the turnip, potato and onion for 5 minutes stirring frequently, until onion is soft.

Spicy Hot and Sour Soup

Remove vegetables from pan with a slotted spoon. Remove pan from heat and stir in flour. Cook for 1 minute. Off the heat, gradually stir in stock. Return pan to heat and bring to the boil. Cook for 2 minutes. Return vegetables to the pan and add salt, pepper, bay leaf and nutmeg. Reduce heat to low, cover and simmer for 20 minutes.

Strain the soup, pressing vegetables to extract juices. Discard contents of strainer. Rinse out saucepan and return strained soup. Place pan over low heat. Stir in cream and cook for 3 minutes. Ladle into individual soup bowls and serve at once, sprinkled with grated carrot.

MUSHROOM SOUP

Metric/U.K.		U.S.
15g/½oz	Butter	1 Tbsp
	Small onion, finely	
½	chopped	½
4 tsp	Flour	4 tsp
	Salt and black pepper	
small		small
pinch	Dried oregano	pinch
small		small
pinch	Cayenne pepper	pinch
450ml/¾ pint	Chicken stock	2 cups
	Mushrooms, wiped	
	clean, trimmed and	
¼kg/½lb	sliced	2 cups
1	Bay leaf	1
5 Tbsp	Double (heavy) cream	5 Tbsp

Mushroom Soup

In a large saucepan melt the butter and fry the onion for 3 minutes until soft. Remove pan from heat and stir in flour, salt, pepper, oregano and cayenne. Cook for 1 minute. Off the heat gradually stir in stock. Stir in mushrooms and add bay leaf.

Return pan to heat, and bring to the boil, stirring constantly. Reduce heat to low, cover and simmer for 30 minutes. Uncover the pan, stir in cream and cook stirring for 2 minutes.

Remove and discard bay leaf. Ladle soup into individual soup bowls and serve at once.

OATMEAL AND CARROT SOUP

A lovely thick soup to warm a winters day.

Metric/U.K.		U.S.
15g/½oz	Butter	1 Tbsp
1	Leek, white part only, sliced	1
¼kg/½lb	Carrots, scraped and thinly sliced	½lb
600ml/1 pint	Chicken stock	2½ cups
	Salt and black pepper	
1	Bouquet garni	1
¼ tsp	Grated orange zest	¼ tsp
15g/½oz	Fine oatmeal mixed with 3 Tbsp milk	2 Tbsp
3 Tbsp	Double (heavy) cream	3 Tbsp
1 Tbsp	Chopped watercress	1 Tbsp

In a large saucepan, melt the butter and fry the leek for 5 minutes until soft. Add carrots and fry for a further 5 minutes, stirring from time to time. Add stock, salt, pepper, bouquet garni and orange zest. Bring to the boil, reduce heat to low, cover and simmer for 30 minutes.

Stir in oatmeal mixture a little at a time. Cook for a further 15 minutes, stirring from time to time, until soup has thickened slightly. Remove and discard bouquet garni.

Stir in cream and cook for 1 minute. Do not allow soup to boil. Ladle soup into individual soup bowls and serve at once, sprinkled with watercress.

JELLIED BEETROOT (BEET) SOUP

The consommé is warmed to make it runny enough to combine smoothly with the other soup ingredients. After chilling, the original consistency will return.

Metric/U.K.		U.S.
300ml/½ pint	Canned condensed beef consommé, warmed	1¼ cups
2 tsp	Sherry	2 tsp
175g/6oz	Beetroots (beets), cooked, peeled and finely chopped	6oz
5 Tbsp	Sour cream	5 Tbsp
2 tsp	Chopped fresh chives	2 tsp

Combine consommé, sherry and beetroots (beets) in a mixing bowl. Beat in the sour cream with a wire whisk until mixture is smooth.

Ladle soup into 2 individual soup bowls.

Chill in the refrigerator for at least 2 hours, or until the soup has set.

Break up the jellied soup with a fork and sprinkle with chives before serving.

Oatmeal and Carrot Soup

CHERVIL SOUP

Chervil looks a little like parsley, and has a very delicate aniseed flavour.

Metric/U.K.		U.S.
15g/½oz	Butter	1 Tbsp
1	Small onion, finely chopped	1
4 tsp	Flour	4 tsp
600ml/1 pint	Chicken stock	2½ cups
25g/1oz	Fresh chervil, finely chopped	⅓ cup
a pinch	Ground mace	a pinch
	Salt and white pepper	
a pinch	celery salt	a pinch

In a large saucepan, melt the butter and fry onion for 5 minutes or until soft. Remove pan from heat and stir in flour. Cook for 1 minute stirring constantly. Off the heat gradually stir in chicken stock. Stir in chervil, mace, salt, pepper and celery salt.

Return pan to heat and bring to the boil stirring constantly. Reduce heat to low,

cover and simmer for 30 minutes, stirring from time to time.

Ladle soup into individual soup bowls and serve at once.

HUNGARIAN FISH SOUP

Fish stock cubes can be bought at some delicatessen, but a stock you have made yourself will improve the flavour of the soup immensely. Ask your fish merchant for fish pieces, which will include all sorts of fish at a very low price. Simmer ½ kg/1 lb of these with 900 ml/1½ pint (1 quart) water, 1 bouquet garni, seasoning, small onion and 2 celery stalks for 2 hours. Strain and use.

Metric/U.K.		U.S.
600ml/1 pint	Fish stock	2½ cups
	Large onion, finely	
1	chopped	1
	Salt and black pepper	
1 tsp	Paprika	1 tsp
	White fish fillets,	
	cut into bite-sized	
¼kg/½lb	pieces	½lb
¼ tsp	Chilli powder	¼ tsp
	Small green pepper,	
	pith removed, seeded	
½	and sliced	½
2 Tbsp	Sour cream	2 Tbsp

In a large saucepan bring the stock to the boil. Reduce heat to low and add onion, salt, pepper and paprika, stirring to blend. Cover and simmer for 1 hour. Strain the mixture, pressing onion to extract juices. Discard contents of strainer. Rinse out saucepan and return strained stock.

Add fish, chilli powder and green pepper. Bring to the boil over moderate heat. Reduce heat to low, cover and simmer for 15 minutes.

Ladle soup into individual soup bowls, stir in sour cream and serve at once.

SPLIT PEA SOUP

Metric/U.K.		U.S.
½ Tbsp	Butter	½ Tbsp
	Lean belly of pork,	
100g/¼lb	chopped	¼lb
1	Garlic clove, crushed	1
	Split peas, soaked	
¼kg/½lb	overnight and drained	1 cup
1 litre/1¼ pints	Chicken stock	3 cups
1 Tbsp	Lemon juice	1 Tbsp
100ml/4floz	Water	½ cup
	Salt and black pepper	
¼ tsp	Dried marjoram	¼ tsp
¼ tsp	Dried oregano	¼ tsp
a pinch	Dried thyme	a pinch
4 Tbsp	Single (light) cream	4 Tbsp

In a large saucepan melt the butter and fry the pork, stirring frequently, for 8 minutes or until golden brown. Add garlic and cook for 1 minute, stirring frequently. Add split peas and stir to coat with fat.

Pour in stock, lemon juice and water and stir in salt, pepper, marjoram, oregano and thyme. Bring to the boil, stirring constantly. Reduce heat to low, cover and simmer for 1 hour or until peas are very soft and soup is smooth. Stir in cream and simmer for 3 minutes. Ladle soup into individual soup bowls and serve at once.

PISTOU

A famous Italian soup, flavoured with fresh basil and garlic.

Metric/U.K.		U.S.
450ml/¾ pint	Water	2 cups
	Salt	
	French (green) beans,	
¼kg/½lb	trimmed and chopped	⅔ cup
	Medium-sized potatoes,	
2	peeled and cubed	2
	Canned peeled	
200g/7oz	tomatoes, drained	7oz
	Black pepper	
50g/2oz	Spaghetti	2oz
1	Garlic clove	1
5 tsp	Chopped fresh basil	5 tsp
1 Tbsp	Olive oil	1 Tbsp
25g/1oz	Grated Parmesan cheese	¼ cup

Pour water into a large saucepan, add salt and bring to the boil. Add beans, potatoes, tomatoes and pepper. Reduce heat, cover and simmer for 25 minutes. Uncover pan, add spaghetti and cook for a further 10 minutes.

Meanwhile, place garlic and basil in a mortar and pound with a pestle until well mixed. Add oil and 1 tablespoon of soup and continue pounding until thoroughly combined. When spaghetti is cooked, stir

Opposite page: *Split Pea Soup*

basil mixture into soup. Ladle soup into individual soup bowls and sprinkle with cheese before serving.

CREAM OF CAULIFLOWER SOUP

Metric/U.K.		U.S.
25g/1oz	Butter	2 Tbsp
1	Small onion, finely chopped	1
1	Celery stalk, finely chopped	1
3 Tbsp	Flour	3 Tbsp
	Salt and black pepper	
600ml/1 pint	Chicken stock	2½ cups
1	Small cauliflower, broken into florets and 2 small leaves reserved	1
2 Tbsp	Double (heavy) cream	2 Tbsp
a pinch	Grated nutmeg	a pinch
2 tsp	Chopped parsley	2 tsp

In a large saucepan melt the butter and fry the onion and celery for 5 minutes or until onion is soft. Remove pan from heat and stir in flour, salt and pepper. Cook stirring for 1 minute. Off the heat, gradually stir in the stock. Add cauliflower and reserved leaves. Return pan to heat and bring to the boil, stirring constantly. Reduce heat to low, cover and simmer for 30 minutes, stirring from time to time.

Strain the soup, pressing vegetables to extract juices. Discard contents of strainer. Return soup to pan. Over low heat, stir in cream and cook, stirring for 5 minutes. Ladle soup into individual soup bowls and serve sprinkled with nutmeg and parsley.

VICHYSSOISE

Metric/U.K.		U.S.
50g/2oz	Butter	¼ cup
½kg/1lb	Leeks, trimmed and chopped	1lb
¼kg/½lb	Potatoes, peeled and chopped	½lb

Vichyssoise

Metric/U.K.		U.S.
1	Celery stalk, chopped	1
300ml/½ pint	Chicken stock	1¼ cups
300ml/½ pint	Milk	1¼ cups
	Salt and black pepper	
¼ tsp	Sugar	¼ tsp
a pinch	Grated nutmeg	a pinch
150ml/¼ pint	Double (heavy) cream	⅔ cup

In a large saucepan melt the butter and fry the leeks, potatoes and celery for 5 minutes. Pour in stock and milk and add salt, pepper, sugar and nutmeg. Bring to the boil, reduce the heat to low, cover and simmer for 30 minutes, stirring from time to time.

Strain the soup into a large mixing bowl, pressing vegetables to extract juices. Discard contents of strainer. Stir half the cream into the soup and set aside to cool. Chill in the refrigerator for 4 hours.

To serve, ladle soup into individual serving bowls and pour a little of remaining cream into each.

MINESTRONE

Metric/U.K.		U.S.
	Bacon slice, rind	
1	removed and chopped	1
1	Garlic clove, crushed	1
1	Small onion, sliced	1
600ml/1 pint	Beef stock	2½ cups
1	Small carrot, diced	1
	Dried haricot (navy)	
	beans, soaked overnight,	
	drained and simmered	
	in fresh water for	
25g/1oz	1 hour	3 Tbsp
1	Celery stalk, diced	1
	Small tomatoes,	
2	quartered	2
25g/1oz	Pasta shapes	1oz
1 Tbsp	Grated Parmesan cheese	1 Tbsp
	Salt and black pepper	

In a large saucepan fry the bacon over low heat for 3 minutes. Add garlic and onion, cover and cook for 5 minutes, shaking the pan from time to time. Add stock and bring to boil. Add carrot and beans. Reduce heat to low, cover and simmer for 20 minutes.

Add celery and tomatoes and cook for a further 10 minutes. Bring soup to boil and add pasta. Reduce heat, cover and simmer 6 minutes. Stir in Parmesan and season.

Ladle soup into individual soup bowls and serve at once.

CREAM OF BROCCOLI SOUP

Minestrone

Metric/U.K.		U.S.
	Spring onions	
	(scallions), finely	
6	chopped	6
	Carrot, scraped and	
1	diced	1
1	Celery stalk, diced	1
1	Garlic clove, crushed	1
1	Bay leaf	1
100ml/4floz	Water	½ cup
	Broccoli, cooked,	
175g/6oz	drained and chopped	6oz
	Salt and white pepper	
¼ tsp	Paprika	¼ tsp

Metric/U.K.		U.S.
450ml/¾ pint	Chicken stock	2 cups
100ml/4floz	Single (light) cream	½ cup
3 Tbsp	Cooked long-grain rice	3 Tbsp
2 Tbsp	Sour cream	2 Tbsp

Bring the spring onions (scallions), carrot, celery, garlic, bay leaf and water to the boil in a large saucepan. Reduce the heat to low cover and simmer for 15 minutes. Add broccoli, salt, pepper, paprika and stock. Stirring constantly, cook for 10 minutes.

Strain the soup, pressing vegetables to extract juices. Discard contents of strainer. Pour soup back into saucepan. Over low heat, stir in cream and rice. Cook stirring, for 5 minutes. Ladle soup into individual soup bowl, spoon over sour cream and serve at once.

ONION SOUP

Metric/U.K.		U.S.
2 tsp	Butter	2 tsp
1 Tbsp	Vegetable oil	1 Tbsp
½	Garlic clove, crushed	½
1	Small potato, peeled and chopped	1
4	Medium-sized onions	4
300ml/½ pint	Milk	1¼ cups
300ml/½ pint	Water	1¼ cups
	Salt and black pepper	
small		small
pinch	Dried sage	pinch
small		small
pinch	Dried thyme	pinch
2 tsp	Cornflour (cornstarch)	2 tsp
1½ Tbsp	dissolved in water	1½ Tbsp
50ml/2floz	Single (light) cream	¼ cup

In a medium-sized frying-pan melt the butter with the oil and fry the garlic for 2 minutes, stirring from time to time. Increase heat to moderate and fry potato for 4 minutes until brown.

Thinly slice 1 of the onions and push slices out into rings. Using a slotted spoon, remove potato from pan and drain on absorbent kitchen paper. Add onion rings to pan and fry for 5 minutes until soft. Drain on absorbent kitchen paper.

Chop remaining onions finely. Pour milk and water into a large saucepan. Add salt,

Onion Soup

pepper, sage, thyme, potato and chopped onions. Bring to the boil, reduce heat to low, cover and simmer for 30 minutes.

Strain the soup, pressing vegetables to extract juices. Discard contents of strainer. Rinse out saucepan and return strained soup. Add reserved onion rings and stir in cornflour (cornstarch) mixture. Bring to the boil over moderate heat, stirring constantly. Simmer for 1 minute, stirring.

Stir in cream and cook over low heat for 1 minute. Ladle soup into individual soup bowls and serve at once.

FRENCH ONION SOUP

Metric/U.K.		U.S.
25g/1oz	Butter	2 Tbsp
1	Small onion, finely chopped	1
450ml/$\frac{3}{4}$ pint	Beef stock	2 cups
1	Bay leaf	1
	Salt and black pepper	
40g/1$\frac{1}{2}$oz	Emmenthal cheese, grated	$\frac{1}{3}$ cup
1 Tbsp	Grated Parmesan cheese	1 Tbsp
2	Thick slices French bread, toasted	2

In a large saucepan, melt the butter and fry the onion for 7 minutes or until browned. Add stock, bay leaf, salt and pepper, cover pan and simmer gently for 30 minutes.

Preheat the oven to 200°C/400°F (gas mark 6). Remove bay leaf and ladle soup into 2 individual ovenproof bowls. Mix Emmenthal and Parmesan together. Cover each slice of bread with cheese and float bread on top of soup. Carefully put bowls into the top of the oven and cook for 5 minutes or until cheese is melted and sizzling. Serve at once.

CARROT SOUP

Metric/U.K.		U.S.
25g/1oz	Butter	2 Tbsp
1	Small onion, finely chopped	1
	Carrots, scraped and	

French Onion Soup

Watercress Soup

¼kg/½lb	finely chopped	½lb
	Long-grain rice, soaked	
	in cold water for 30	
1 Tbsp	minutes and drained	1 Tbsp
	Salt and black pepper	
¼ tsp	Sugar	¼ tsp
600ml/1 pint	Chicken stock	2½ cups
2 Tbsp	Double (heavy) cream	2 Tbsp
GARNISH		
	Carrot, scraped and cut	
½	into matchstick strips	½

In a large saucepan melt the butter and fry the onion for 5 minutes until soft. Add carrots, rice, salt, pepper and sugar and cook for a further 3 minutes, stirring. Pour over stock and bring to boil, stirring constantly. Reduce heat to low, cover and simmer for 30 minutes.

Strain the soup, pressing vegetables to extract juices. Discard contents of strainer. Return soup to pan. Over low heat stir in

cream and cook for 5 minutes. Ladle soup into individual soup bowls and serve sprinkled with carrot strips.

WATERCRESS SOUP

Metric/U.K.		U.S.
600ml/1 pint	Milk	2½ cups
	Potatoes, cooked and	
¼kg/½lb	mashed	½ lb
	Salt	
	Bunch watercress,	
1	chopped	1
15g/½oz	Butter	1 Tbsp
4 tsp	Single (light) cream	4 tsp
1 Tbsp	Chopped parsley	1 Tbsp
	Black pepper	

Pour the milk into a large saucepan and bring to the boil over moderate heat. Stir in potatoes and salt until well blended. Stir in watercress and cook for 5 minutes. Remove pan from heat and stir in butter and cream.

Ladle soup into individual soup bowls and serve at once, sprinkled with parsley and pepper.

SCOTCH BROTH

Metric/U.K.		U.S.
	Scrag end of neck of lamb, trimmed of excess	
½kg/1lb	fat and chopped	1lb
600ml/1 pint	Water	2½ cups
	Salt and black pepper	
25g/1oz	Pearl barley, blanched	⅛ cup
	Green split peas, soaked overnight in cold water	
25g/1oz	and drained	⅛ cup
	Small carrot, scraped	
1	and chopped	1
1	Small onion, chopped	1
	Leek, white part only,	
1	chopped	1
1	Celery stalk, chopped	1
	Turnip, peeled and	
½	chopped	½
1 Tbsp	Chopped parsley	1 Tbsp

Put lamb in a large saucepan and pour over water. Bring to the boil and remove scum. Add salt, pepper, barley and peas. Reduce the heat to low, cover and simmer for 1 hour.

Add carrot, onion, leek, celery and turnip and continue cooking for 45 minutes, stirring from time to time.

Remove pan from heat. Remove meat from soup and remove meat from bones. Discard bones and return meat to pan. Cook over moderate heat for 5 minutes, taste and add more seasoning if necessary. Ladle soup into individual soup bowls and serve sprinkled with parsley.

PARSLEY SOUP

Metric/U.K.		U.S.
	Streaky (fatty) bacon slices, rind removed	
3	and finely chopped	3
15g/½oz	Butter	1 Tbsp
	Small onion, finely	
1	chopped	1

1	Small potato, peeled and finely chopped	1
1	Small turnip, peeled and grated	1
1	Bunch parsley, finely chopped	1
	Salt and black pepper	
300ml/½ pint	Chicken stock	1¼ cups
300ml/½ pint	Milk	1¼ cups
75g/3oz	Cheddar cheese, diced	3oz

In a large saucepan fry the bacon over moderate heat for 5 minutes or until browned. Drain bacon on absorbent kitchen paper and keep hot.

Add butter to bacon fat in pan and when melted, fry onion, potato and turnip for 5 minutes or until onion is soft. Add parsley, salt and pepper. Pour in stock and milk and bring to the boil. Reduce heat to low, cover and simmer for 25 minutes.

Strain the soup, pressing vegetables to extract juices. Discard contents of strainer. Rinse out saucepan and return soup to pan. Cook for 2 minutes over moderate heat to reheat.

Ladle soup into individual soup bowls and serve at once, sprinkled with diced cheese and bacon.

SPINACH SOUP

Metric/U.K.		U.S.
15g/½oz	Butter	1 Tbsp
1	Small onion, finely chopped	1
1 Tbsp	Flour	1 Tbsp
600ml/1 pint	Chicken stock	2½ cups
	Salt and black pepper	
¼ tsp	Paprika	¼ tsp
¼ tsp	Grated nutmeg	¼ tsp
1 Tbsp	Lemon juice	1 Tbsp

½kg/1lb	Spinach, trimmed and coarsely chopped	1lb
1½ Tbsp	Double (heavy) cream	1½ Tbsp
3	Lean bacon slices, rinds removed, cooked until crisp and coarsely chopped	3

In a large saucepan melt the butter and fry the onion for 5 minutes until soft. Remove pan from heat and stir in flour. Cook for 1 minute. Off the heat gradually stir in stock, then salt, pepper, paprika, nutmeg, lemon juice and spinach.

Return pan to heat, and bring to the boil, stirring constantly. Reduce heat to low, cover and simmer for 20 minutes.

Remove pan from heat. Ladle soup into an electric blender, a little at a time, and blend until smooth. Return soup to pan and bring to boil slowly, stirring from time to time. Adjust seasoning if necessary. Ladle soup into individual soup bowls, add a little cream to each and sprinkle with bacon before serving.

POTATO SOUP

Metric/U.K.		U.S.
25g/1oz	Butter	2 Tbsp
1 Tbsp	Vegetable oil	1 Tbsp
1	Small onion, finely chopped	1
2	Small leeks, white part only, sliced	2
3	Medium-sized potatoes, peeled and finely chopped	3
	Salt and black pepper	
300ml/½ pint	Chicken stock	1¼ cups
150ml/¼ pint	Milk	⅔ cup

In a large saucepan melt the butter with the oil and fry the onion for 5 minutes or until soft. Add leeks and potatoes and cook, stirring from time to time, for 10 minutes. Add salt, pepper, stock and milk and bring to the boil, stirring. Reduce heat to low, cover and simmer for 25 minutes.

Strain soup, pressing vegetables to extract

Metric/U.K.		U.S.
75ml/3floz	Sour cream	¼ cup
2 Tbsp	Plain yoghurt	2 Tbsp
	Canned tomatoes	
	reduced to purée with	
275g/10oz	can liquid	10oz
1 Tbsp	Lemon juice	1 Tbsp
1 tsp	Sugar	1 tsp
	Salt and white pepper	
2	Mint sprigs	2

Put the garlic, sour cream and half the yoghurt into a soup tureen. Stir to mix. Rub the tomato purée through a strainer to remove seeds and stir purée into sour cream mixture.

Add lemon juice, sugar, salt and pepper. Chill in the refrigerator for 4 hours before serving.

Just before serving, stir in remaining yoghurt, garnish with mint springs and serve.

MINT AND MUSHROOM SOUP

Metric/U.K.		U.S.
	Large potatoes, peeled	
2	and coarsely chopped	2
½	Small onion	½
450ml/¾ pint	Chicken stock	2 cups
	Grated zest and juice of	
	½ lemon	
½ tsp	Dried rosemary	½ tsp
	Salt and black pepper	
25g/1oz	Butter	2 Tbsp
	Mushrooms, wiped	
100g/¼lb	clean and sliced	1 cup
2 tsp	Flour	2 tsp
	Finely chopped fresh	
1 Tbsp	mint	1 Tbsp
5 Tbsp	Double (heavy) cream	5 Tbsp

Place potatoes, onion, stock, lemon zest and juice, rosemary, salt and pepper in a large saucepan. Bring to the boil, reduce heat to low, cover and simmer for 25 minutes, stirring from time to time.

Meanwhile, melt the butter in a small saucepan and fry the mushrooms, stirring from time to time, for 5 minutes. Sprinkle over the flour and stir into mushroom mixture. Remove from heat and set aside.

Remove potatoes and onion from stock and rub through a strainer. Return purée to stock. Add mushrooms to stock, increase heat and bring to the boil, stirring con-

Iced Tomato Soup

juices. Discard contents of strainer. Return soup to pan and cook over low heat for 5 minutes, stirring from time to time. Ladle into individual soup bowls and serve at once.

ICED TOMATO SOUP

Metric/U.K.		U.S.
	Small garlic clove,	
1	crushed	1

stantly. Stir in mint and remove pan from heat. Ladle into individual soup bowls and swirl in cream just before serving.

VEGETABLE SOUP

Metric/U.K.		U.S.
15g/½oz	Butter	1 Tbsp
1	Large carrot, scraped and diced	1
¼	Small swede (rutabaga) peeled and diced	¼
1	Small leek, trimmed and chopped	1
1	Small potato, peeled and diced	1
1	Celery stalk, chopped	1
2	Tomatoes, blanched, skinned and chopped	2
25g/1oz	Dried butter (lima) beans, soaked overnight and drained	3 Tbsp
	Salt and black pepper	
600ml/1 pint	Beef stock	2½ cups
1	Bay leaf	1
25g/1oz	Frozen peas, thawed	3 Tbsp
1 tsp	Chopped parsley	1 tsp

In a large saucepan melt the butter and cook the carrot, swede (rutabaga), leek, potato, and celery for 10 minutes, stirring from time to time.

Add tomatoes, butter (lima) beans, salt and pepper and pour in stock. Add bay leaf, increase heat and bring to the boil, stirring constantly. Reduce heat to low, cover and simmer for 20 minutes.

Strain the soup into a large mixing bowl. Remove and discard the bay leaf. Add half the vegetables in the strainer to the strained stock. Rub remaining vegetables through strainer into a small mixing bowl. Rinse out saucepan and add purée. Stir in stock and vegetable mixture. Add peas and bring to the boil, stirring frequently. Reduce heat, cover and simmer for 5 minutes.

Ladle soup into individual soup bowls and serve at once, sprinkled with parsley. *Vegetable Soup*

VEGETABLES

MATCHSTICK POTATOES

The potatoes are first soaked in water to remove excess starch (starch absorbs the oil and could make the potatoes unpleasantly soggy). Double-frying also ensures crisp results.

Metric/U.K.		U.S.
½kg/1lb	Potatoes	1lb
	Oil for deep-frying	
	Salt	

Peel potatoes and cut into matchstick strips. Place in a large bowl and cover with cold water. Set aside for 30 minutes.

Drain potatoes on absorbent kitchen paper. Heat a deep pan one-third full of oil to 180°C/350°F. Put the potatoes in a deep-frying basket, a few at a time, and lower into the oil. Fry for 3 minutes. Drain on absorbent kitchen paper.

When all the potatoes are fried, increase temperature of oil to 190°C/375°F. Put all potatoes back into basket and fry again, shaking the basket, for 1 minute.

Drain on absorbent kitchen paper, sprinkle with salt and serve very hot.

ANISEED CARROTS

Metric/U.K.		U.S.
	Soft (light) brown	
1 tsp	sugar	1 tsp
25g/1oz	Butter	2 Tbsp
1 tsp	Aniseed	1 tsp
	Salt and black pepper	
350g/¾lb	Small carrots, scraped	¾lb

Put the sugar, butter, aniseed, salt and pepper in to a saucepan over low heat. When the mixture begins to bubble, add the carrots. Stir well, reduce the heat to

Matchstick Potatoes

low, cover and simmer for 15 minutes.
Serve very hot.

SPINACH WITH CHEESE

Spinach has a very high water content so extract as much water as possible after cooking, or your finished dish will be swimming in excess liquid.

Metric/U.K.		U.S.
	Spinach, trimmed washed and coarsely	
½kg/1lb	chopped	1lb
	Salt	
50g/2oz	Butter	¼ cup
50g/2oz	Cheddar cheese, grated	½ cup
	Black pepper	

Put spinach in a large saucepan with the water it was washed in still clinging to the leaves. Add salt to taste and bring to the boil over moderately high heat. Reduce heat to low, cover and simmer for 7 minutes. Drain in a colander, pressing down with a wooden spoon to extract excess liquid.

In a large frying-pan melt the butter and add spinach. Gradually stir in three-quarters of cheese and cook over moderate heat for 2 minutes, stirring. Season with pepper and more salt if wished.

Place spinach mixture in a flameproof dish. Sprinkle over remaining cheese and cook under a hot grill (broiler) for 5 minutes until cheese is golden and bubbling. Serve at once.

BEAN SPROUTS WITH GINGER

Metric/U.K.		U.S.
2 Tbsp	Oil	2 Tbsp
	Small onion, finely	
1	sliced	1
	Fresh root ginger,	
1·5 cm/½in	peeled and cut into	
piece	thin strips	½ in piece
	Salt	
¼kg/½lb	Bean sprouts	½lb

In a large frying-pan heat the oil and fry the onion over low heat for 5 minutes until soft. Add ginger and fry for further 3 minutes.

Aniseed Carrots

Add salt and bean sprouts and stir to mix. Increase the heat to moderately high and fry the bean sprouts for 2 minutes, stirring constantly. Serve at once.

FENNEL IN CHEESE SAUCE

Metric/U.K.		U.S.
	Head of fennel,	
	trimmed and cut into	
½	5 cm/2in lengths	½
	Cheese sauce (see page	
300ml/½ pint	13)	1¼ cups
1 Tbsp	Grated Parmesan cheese	1 Tbsp
25g/1oz	Dry white breadcrumbs	¼ cup
15g/½oz	Butter	1 Tbsp

Preheat the oven to 180°C 350°F (gas mark 4). Place fennel in the top half of a steamer and steam over simmering water for 15 minutes. Transfer fennel to an ovenproof dish.

Pour the cheese sauce over the fennel and sprinkle with Parmesan and breadcrumbs. Dot with butter.

Bake for 15 to 20 minutes or until top is golden brown and sauce is bubbling. Serve at once.

HARVARD BEETS

Freshly cooked beetroots (beets) will be a pleasant surprise to those who only know the taste of the vinegar-soaked type. This recipe is a famous American invention.

Metric/U.K.		U.S.
25g/1oz	Sugar	2 Tbsp
½ tsp	Cornflour (cornstarch)	½ tsp
2 Tbsp	Malt vinegar	2 Tbsp
50ml/2floz	Water	¼ cup
	Beetroot (beets),	
¼kg/½lb	cooked and sliced	½lb

Combine the sugar and cornflour (cornstarch) in a cup. In a medium-sized saucepan, heat the vinegar and water together over low heat, until just lukewarm. Gradually add sugar mixture, stirring constantly until sugar has dissolved. Bring to the boil and cook, stirring for 1 minute until smooth.

Add beetroot (beets) and stir. Reduce heat to low and simmer for 5 minutes until heated through. Serve at once.

ROAST POTATO FANS

Simple to make and very attractive.

Metric/U.K.		U.S.
	Medium-sized potatoes,	
4	peeled	4

Roast Potato Fans

25g/1oz	Butter	2 Tbsp
	Salt and black pepper	
1 Tbsp	Dry white breadcrumbs	1 Tbsp

Make 6 mm/¼ inch wide cuts across potatoes, but do not cut completely through. Put potatoes into a large bowl, cover with cold water and set aside.

Preheat the oven to 200°C/400°F (gas mark 6). Grease an ovenproof dish large enough to take the potatoes in one layer with one-quarter of the butter. Drain potatoes on absorbent kitchen paper and place in dish, cut sides up. Dot each potato with remaining butter and sprinkle with salt and pepper. Bake for 45 minutes, basting from time to time.

Sprinkle over breadcrumbs and bake for further 15 minutes. Serve at once.

MARINATED MUSHROOMS

Metric/U.K.		U.S.
	Small button	
	mushrooms, stalks	
	trimmed and wiped	
100g/¼lb	clean	1 cup
MARINADE		
	Salt and black pepper	
¼ tsp	Dried dill	¼ tsp
1 Tbsp	Tarragon vinegar	1 Tbsp
1 tsp	Lemon juice	1 tsp
1 Tbsp	Olive oil	1 Tbsp

Combine all the marinade ingredients in a shallow mixing bowl. Add mushrooms and stir to coat with marinade. Cover dish and set aside in a cool place for 2 hours, basting frequently.

Drain off and discard marinade and pile mushrooms in a small serving dish. Serve at once.

TURNIPS WITH CHEESE AND BREADCRUMBS

Metric/U.K.		U.S.
	Turnips, peeled and	
½kg/1lb	sliced	1lb
	Small onion, sliced	
	and pushed out into	
1	rings	1
1	Garlic clove, crushed	1
	Salt and black pepper	

Metric/U.K.		U.S.
1 Tbsp	Chopped parsley	1 Tbsp
50ml/2floz	Chicken stock	¼ cup
15g/½oz	Butter	1 Tbsp
1 Tbsp	Dry white breadcrumbs	1 Tbsp
25g/1oz	Grated Parmesan cheese	¼ cup

Preheat the oven to 190°C/375°F (gas mark 5).

Lightly grease an ovenproof dish. Place one-third of turnip slices in bottom of dish. Cover with half the onion rings and half the garlic. Sprinkle with half the salt, pepper and parsley. Continue making layers, ending with a layer of turnip. Pour over stock and dot with butter. Sprinkle over breadcrumbs and Parmesan. Bake for 40 to 50 minutes until turnips are tender. Serve at once.

ONIONS WITH SOUR CREAM

Metric/U.K.		U.S.
4	Streaky (fatty) bacon slices, rinds removed and chopped	4
4	Medium-sized onions, sliced and pushed out into rings	4
	Salt and black pepper	
1 tsp	Paprika	1 tsp
1 tsp	Dried dill	1 tsp
100ml/4floz	Sour cream	½ cup

In a medium-sized frying-pan fry the bacon over moderately high heat for 5 minutes. Drain bacon on absorbent kitchen paper and keep hot.

Add onions, salt, pepper and paprika to fat in the pan. Fry for 5 minutes or until onions are soft, stirring from time to time. Stir in dill and sour cream and cook for 3 minutes, stirring.

Spoon mixture into a serving dish and sprinkle with bacon before serving.

PURÉED PARSNIPS

Metric/U.K.		U.S.
3	Large parsnips, cooked and kept hot	3
40g/1½oz	Butter	3 Tbsp
	Salt and black pepper	
½ Tbsp	Chopped parsley	½ Tbsp

Gently rub the parsnips through a strainer into a medium-sized saucepan. Discard contents of strainer.

Add butter, salt and pepper. Cook gently over low heat, stirring frequently, for 2 minutes or until heated through.

Stir in parsley, transfer to a serving dish and serve at once.

PEAS WITH BACON AND ONIONS

Metric/U.K.		U.S.
	Streaky (fatty) bacon slices, rinds removed	
2	and chopped	2
½ Tbsp	Butter	½ Tbsp
	Small white onions,	
3	finely chopped	3
1 Tbsp	Flour	1 Tbsp
	Salt and black pepper	
100ml/4floz	Chicken stock	½ cup
1	Bouquet garni	1
¼kg/½lb	Frozen peas, thawed	½lb

In a medium-sized saucepan fry the bacon over moderately high heat for 5 minutes. Drain the bacon on absorbent kitchen paper and set aside.

Reduce heat and add butter. Fry the onions for 8 minutes until brown, stirring. Remove pan from heat. Remove onions from pan and add to bacon. Stir in flour and cook for 1 minute. Season with salt and pepper. Off the heat, gradually add the stock. Add bouquet garni and reserved bacon and onions. Return pan to heat.

Bring to the boil, stirring constantly. Stir in peas and reduce heat to low. Cover and simmer for 5 minutes, stirring from time to time.

Remove and discard bouquet garni and serve at once.

PURÉED BROCCOLI

Metric/U.K.		U.S.
	Broccoli, trimmed, cooked and drained with 2 Tbsp cooking	
¼kg/½lb	liquid reserved	½ lb
50g/2oz	Butter	¼ cup
a pinch	Grated nutmeg	a pinch
½ tsp	Chopped parsley	½ tsp
	Black pepper	
2 Tbsp	Double (heavy) cream	2 Tbsp

Moisten broccoli with the reserved cooking liquid and purée in an electric blender.

In a large frying-pan melt the butter and add broccoli purée, nutmeg, parsley and pepper and stir well to mix. Cook over moderate heat for 1 minute. Remove pan from heat and stir in cream. Serve at once.

MARROW (SQUASH) BAKE

Marrow (squash) is a glut vegetable and if you grow your own, it is often a difficult job to think of new ways to cook it. Marrow (squash) tends to be rather bland, so season well and add mace to taste. Grated nutmeg may be used instead of mace. There will be about 350g ¾lb loss in weight after peeling and seeding.

Metric/U.K.		U.S.
	1 vegetable marrow	
1kg/2lb	(squash)	2lb
25g/1oz	Butter	2 Tbsp
225ml/8floz	White sauce (see page 12)	1 cup
	Salt and black pepper	
	Ground mace	
1	Egg yolk	1
1	Egg white, stiffly beaten	1
	Fresh white	
15g/½oz	breadcrumbs	¼ cup

Peel the marrow (squash) and slice in half. Scoop out and discard the seeds. Cut flesh into 2.5 cm/1 inch cubes.

Preheat oven to 180°C/350°F (gas mark 4). Grease a large ovenproof dish and set aside.

In a large frying-pan melt the butter and fry the marrow (squash) for 15 minutes over moderate heat. Place marrow and buttery juices in an electric blender and purée. Scrape purée into a large mixing bowl and beat in white sauce, salt, pepper, mace and egg yolk. Fold in egg white. Spoon mixture into prepared dish and sprinkle with breadcrumbs.

Bake for 30 minutes until golden brown on top. Serve at once.

PARSLEY POTATOES

Metric/U.K.		U.S.
½kg/1lb	New potatoes, scrubbed	1lb
	Salt	

Peas with Bacon and Onions

Parsley Potatoes

Scoop out the insides to within 6mm/ ¼ inch of the shell, being careful not to pierce the skin. Place the flesh in a mixing bowl and the potato shells in a grill (broiler) pan. Prepare chosen filling and spoon into shells. Place filled potatoes under a hot grill (broiler) and grill (broil) for 5 to 8 minutes until golden brown on top.

FILLING 1

Metric/U.K.		U.S.
	Flesh from potatoes	
2	baked in jackets	2
25g/1oz	Brie cheese	1oz
¼ tsp	Dried chives	¼ tsp
	Salt	
1	Small egg yolk	1
25g/1oz	Butter, softened	2 Tbsp

Beat all the ingredients together until thoroughly mixed.

FILLING 2

Metric/U.K.		U.S.
	Flesh from potatoes	
2	baked in jackets	2
25g/1oz	Gorgonzola cheese, crumbled	¼ cup
½ Tbsp	Single (light) cream	½ Tbsp
1 tsp	Tomato purée (paste)	1 tsp
	Black pepper	
¼ tsp	Dried basil	¼ tsp
25g/1oz	Butter, softened	2 Tbsp

Beat all the ingredients together until thoroughly mixed.

FILLING 3

Metric/U.K.		U.S.
	Flesh from potatoes	
2	baked in jackets	2
	Cheshire cheese,	
50g/2oz	crumbled	½ cup
	Small dessert apple, peeled, cored and	
½	finely chopped	½
½ tsp	French mustard	½ tsp
	Salt	
25g/1oz	Butter, softened	2 Tbsp

Beat all the ingredients together until thoroughly mixed.

25g/1oz	Butter	2 Tbsp
2 Tbsp	Chopped parsley	2 Tbsp

Cook the potatoes in a little salted water for 15 to 20 minutes until tender. Drain and carefully peel off skins. Transfer potatoes to a warmed serving dish and keep hot.

Melt the butter in a small saucepan and stir in the parsley. Spoon butter mixture over potatoes. Using 2 large spoons, toss potatoes to coat in butter. Serve at once.

STUFFED BAKED POTATOES

The ever-versatile potato makes a really appetizing vegetable stuffed and baked. Served with a salad, it can easily go to the table as a light lunch or supper.

Allow one potato per person. The amount of fillings given here is enough to fill 2 large potatoes.

To prepare the potatoes, bake in the oven and place on a board. Remove a thin slice from one top flat side of the potato.

FILLING 4

Metric/U.K.		U.S.
	Flesh from potatoes	
2	baked in jackets	2
50g/2oz	Cheddar cheese, grated	½ cup
1 tsp	Chutney	1 tsp
	Small celery stalk,	
1	finely chopped	1
25g/1oz	Butter, softened	2 Tbsp

Beat all the ingredients together until thoroughly mixed.

FILLING 5

Metric/U.K.		U.S.
	Flesh from potatoes	
2	baked in jackets	2
	Streaky (fatty) bacon	
	slices, grilled (broiled)	
2	and crumbled	2
15g/½oz	Butter	1 Tbsp
	Mushrooms, wiped	

50g/2oz	clean and chopped	⅓ cup
	Salt and black pepper	

Combine potato flesh and bacon. In a frying-pan melt butter and fry mushrooms for 2 minutes, stirring. Add mushrooms and buttery juices to potato mixture. Add salt and pepper and beat until thoroughly mixed

FILLING 6

Metric/U.K.		U.S.
	Flesh from potatoes	
2	baked in jackets	2
	Shrimp, shelled	
50g/2oz	(peeled)	⅓ cup
	Spring onions	
2	(scallions), chopped	2
¼ tsp	Grated lemon zest	¼ tsp
¼ tsp	Chopped parsley	¼ tsp
⅛ tsp	Cayenne pepper	⅛ tsp
25g/1oz	Butter, softened	2 Tbsp

Beat all the ingredients together until thoroughly mixed.

Baked Potatoes, with six very different fillings

59

COURGETTES (ZUCCHINI) WITH CAULIFLOWER

Metric/U.K.		U.S.
3	Medium-sized courgettes (zucchini), trimmed sliced and dégorged	3
½	Medium-sized cauliflower, trimmed and broken into florets	½
75ml/3floz	Olive oil	⅓ cup
1 Tbsp	Turmeric	1 Tbsp
	Salt	

Preheat the oven to 190°C, 375°F (gas mark 5). Cook the courgettes and cauliflower in boiling salted water for 3 minutes. Drain and set aside.

Pour the oil into a roasting tin and set over moderate heat until hot. Off the heat stir in turmeric and salt. Stir in vegetable mixture until well coated with oil mixture. Roast vegetables for 30 minutes, turning in oil from time to time.

Drain off excess oil and arrange vegetables in a serving dish. Serve at once.

BROCCOLI WITH ALMONDS

Metric/U.K.		U.S.
¼kg/½lb	Broccoli, trimmed, cooked, drained and kept hot	½lb
25g/1oz	Butter	2 Tbsp
2 Tbsp	Chopped toasted almonds	2 Tbsp
1 Tbsp	Lemon juice	1 Tbsp

Broccoli with Almonds

Arrange the cooked broccoli in a serving dish. Dot with butter and sprinkle with the toasted almonds. Sprinkle over the lemon juice and serve at once.

LEEKS PROVENÇAL

It is far better to steam, rather than boil, leeks. Open steam in a flower steamer (see Asparagus page 16) for 20 minutes.

Metric/U.K.		U.S.
6	Small whole young leeks, cooked and kept hot	6

stirring constantly, or until tomatoes are pulped. Remove pan from heat and stir in sugar and lemon juice. Season with salt and pepper. Pour sauce over leeks and serve at once.

Left: *Corn Bake;*
Above: *Leeks Provençal*

CORN BAKE

Metric/U.K.		U.S.
2	Eggs	2
1 Tbsp	Flour	1 Tbsp
150ml/¼ pint	Single (light) cream	⅔ cup
25g/1oz	Butter, melted	2 Tbsp
	Salt and black pepper	
	Frozen sweetcorn,	
¼kg/½lb	thawed	½lb

Preheat oven to 180°C/350°F (gas mark 4). Grease a shallow ovenproof dish and set aside.

In a large mixing bowl, whisk the eggs until light and frothy. Stir in flour, cream and butter. Add salt, pepper and sweetcorn and stir for 1 minute. Pour mixture into dish and bake for 1 to 1¼ hours or until a fine warm skewer inserted in the centre comes out clean. Serve at once.

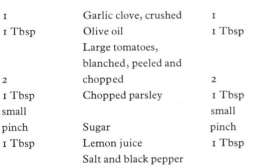

1	Garlic clove, crushed	1
1 Tbsp	Olive oil	1 Tbsp
	Large tomatoes,	
	blanched, peeled and	
2	chopped	2
1 Tbsp	Chopped parsley	1 Tbsp
small		small
pinch	Sugar	pinch
1 Tbsp	Lemon juice	1 Tbsp
	Salt and black pepper	

Arrange the leeks in a serving dish, set aside and keep hot.

Place garlic in a small saucepan and add oil, tomatoes and parsley. Cook over moderately high heat for 2 minutes,

Above: *Corn on the Cob, with lots of butter;* Opposite page: *Walnut Cauliflower*

CORN ON THE COB

Salt should never be added to the cooking water as it tends to toughen the sweet kernels. This recipe is for fresh corn, but frozen may be used, in which case follow the packet instructions for cooking times. Serve as an accompaniment to chops or steaks, or even as a light meal.

Metric/U.K.		U.S.
2	Corn ears, husks and threads removed	2
¼ tsp	Sugar	¼ tsp
	Butter	
	Black pepper	

Half-fill a large saucepan with hot water and add the sugar. Place pan over high heat and bring to the boil. Place corn in pan, reduce heat to moderate, cover and simmer for 10 to 20 minutes, depending on the age of the corn. The corn is cooked when the kernels feel tender when tested with the point of a knife and have turned bright yellow.

Drain well and serve at once liberally sprinkled with pepper and plenty of butter.

WALNUT CAULIFLOWER

Metric/U.K.		U.S.
15g/½oz	Butter	1 Tbsp
15g/½oz	Flour	2 Tbsp
225ml/8floz	Milk	1 cup
100ml/4floz	Single (light) cream	½ cup
1	Small egg, lightly beaten	1
2 Tbsp	Cider vinegar	2 Tbsp
1 Tbsp	Soft (light) brown sugar	1 Tbsp
1 Tbsp	French mustard	1 Tbsp
50g/2oz	Walnuts, chopped and toasted	⅓ cup
1	Small cauliflower, cooked and kept hot	1

In a medium-sized saucepan, melt the butter. Remove pan from heat and stir in flour. Cook for 1 minute. Off the heat, gradually stir in milk and cream. Add egg, vinegar, sugar and mustard. Return pan to low heat and cook for 1 minute, stirring. Do not allow to boil or egg will scramble. Stir in walnuts and cook for a further 1 minute, stirring.

Place cauliflower in a warmed serving dish, pour over sauce and serve at once.

*Brussels Sprouts
Polonaise*

BRUSSELS SPROUTS WITH GRAPES

Metric/U.K.		U.S.
25g/1oz	Butter	2 Tbsp
	Brussels sprouts, trimmed, cooked and	
350g/¾lb	kept hot	¾lb
	Salt and black pepper	
175g/6oz	Seedless green grapes	6oz

In a medium-sized saucepan, melt the butter and add sprouts, salt and pepper. Mix well to coat the sprouts in butter.

Add the grapes and cook gently until sprouts and grapes are thoroughly heated. Serve at once.

BRUSSELS SPROUTS POLONAISE

Metric/U.K.		U.S.
	Brussels sprouts, trimmed, cooked and	
350g/¾lb	kept hot	¾lb
	Egg, hard-boiled (hard-cooked) and finely	
1	chopped	1
1 Tbsp	Chopped parsley	1 Tbsp
	Salt and black pepper	
25g/1oz	Butter	2 Tbsp
	Fresh white	
25g/1oz	breadcrumbs	½ cup

Arrange the Brussels sprouts in a heated serving dish. Sprinkle with the egg, parsley, salt and pepper. Set aside and keep hot.

Melt the butter in a small saucepan and add the breadcrumbs. Cook over moderate heat for 5 minutes or until the breadcrumbs are golden, stirring from time to time.

Sprinkle browned breadcrumbs over sprouts and serve at once.

CARROTS VICHY

Metric/U.K.		U.S.
25g/1oz	Butter	2 Tbsp
	Small young carrots, scraped and thinly	
½kg/1lb	sliced	1lb
½ tsp	Sugar	½ tsp
	Salt and black pepper	
1 Tbsp	Chopped parsley	1 Tbsp

In a large frying-pan melt the butter over

moderate heat. Add carrots, sugar, salt and pepper and cook over low heat for 10 minutes or until carrots are tender but still crisp, shaking pan from time to time.

Serve at once, sprinkled with chopped parsley.

ONIONS TURBIGO

Metric/U.K.		U.S.
	Medium-sized Spanish (Bermuda)	
2	onions	2
1	Frankfurter, chopped	1
1 Tbsp	Tomato purée (paste)	1 Tbsp
25g/1oz	Butter	2 Tbsp
	Salt and black pepper	

Preheat the oven to 180°C/350°F (gas mark 4). Using a sharp knife, remove centre sections of onions, leaving 3 outer layers of onion to form a shell. Chop the onion centres and place in a bowl. Add the frankfurter, tomato purée (paste), salt and pepper to the onion.

Pile the mixture back into the onion shells. Melt half the butter and brush 2 pieces of foil. Place one onion on each piece of foil. Dot with remaining butter and crimp edges of foil to make parcels. Cook for 1½ hours. Remove foil and place in a serving dish. Serve at once.

COURGETTES (ZUCCHINI) À LA GRECQUE

Metric/U.K.		U.S.
¼kg/½lb	Courgettes (zucchini), trimmed and sliced	½lb
1	Small onion, finely chopped	1
4	Coriander seeds, crushed	4
2 Tbsp	Lemon juice	2 Tbsp
2 Tbsp	Olive oil	2 Tbsp
1 small	Bay leaf	1 small
pinch	Dried thyme	pinch
	Salt and black pepper	
150ml/¼ pint	Water	⅔ cup

Put all the ingredients into a medium-sized saucepan and bring to the boil. Reduce the heat to low, cover and simmer for 15

minutes.

Remove the lid and simmer for further 10 minutes or until most of the liquid has been absorbed. Using a slotted spoon, transfer vegetables to a serving dish. If there is too much liquid, boil to reduce. Remove bay leaf and pour sauce over vegetables. Allow to cool, then chill in the refrigerator for 30 minutes before serving.

BAKED STUFFED AUBERGINES (EGGPLANTS)

Metric/U.K.		U.S.
1	Large aubergine (egg plant), trimmed, halved and dégorged	1
2 Tbsp	Olive oil	2 Tbsp
1	Small onion, finely chopped	1
1	Garlic clove, crushed	1
25g/1oz	Butter	2 Tbsp
175g/6oz	Mushrooms, wiped clean and chopped	1½ cups
	Salt and black pepper	
50g/2oz	Cottage cheese	¼ cup
1 Tbsp	Chopped parsley	1 Tbsp
1 Tbsp	Grated Parmesan cheese	1 Tbsp

Courgettes (Zucchini) à la Grecque

	Fresh white	
2 Tbsp	breadcrumbs	2 Tbsp

Squeeze the aubergine (eggplant) halves gently to remove as much liquid as possible and dry on absorbent kitchen paper. Put aubergine (eggplant) halves in a flameproof dish, skin side down, and pour over half the oil. Pour a little water in the dish to just cover the bottom. Cook under a moderate grill (broiler) for 10 minutes until soft. Scoop out flesh into a bowl, leaving skins intact. Chop the flesh.

Preheat the oven to 200°C/400°F (gas mark 6). Heat remaining oil in a frying-pan and fry onion and garlic over low heat for 5 minutes. Add the butter to the pan and then the mushrooms. Fry gently for a further 5 minutes. Season with salt and pepper. Remove from heat and stir in aubergine (eggplant) flesh, cottage cheese and parsley. Fill shells with mixture and sprinkle with Parmesan and breadcrumbs.

Grease a clean flameproof dish and put in aubergine (eggplant) halves. Cover with foil and bake for 20 minutes. Remove foil and cook for a further 10 minutes until topping is golden brown. Serve at once.

Stuffed Aubergines *(Eggplants)*

BRAISED CELERY

A frying pan is used here to enable the celery to lie flat while it is being cooked. A wide, shallow saucepan can also be used. The strained cooking liquid may be made into an accompanying sauce: melt 15g/½oz (1 Tbsp) butter and stir in 2 Tbsp flour. Cook for 1 minute. Off the heat, gradually stir in the strained liquid. Cook, stirring until thickened.

Metric/U.K.		U.S.
2	Streaky (fatty) bacon slices, chopped	2
1	Small carrot, scraped and sliced	1
6	Small whole onions	6
1	Small head of celery, broken into stalks	1
1	Bouquet garni	1
	Salt and black pepper	
450ml/¾ pint	Chicken stock	2 cups

Arrange the bacon, carrot and onions in the bottom of a large frying-pan and place the celery on top. Add bouquet garni, salt, pepper and stock.

Place the pan over moderate heat and bring to the boil. Reduce the heat to low, cover and simmer for 1 hour.

Strain the celery mixture and remove the bouquet garni. Turn into a serving dish and serve at once.

Braised Celery

SALADS

EGG SALAD

Metric/U.K.		U.S.
3	Eggs, hard-boiled (hard-cooked) and sliced	3
1	Small green pepper, pith removed, seeded and finely chopped	1
1	Small red pepper, pith removed, seeded and finely sliced	1
3	Button mushrooms, wiped clean and sliced	3
6	Black (pitted) olives, stoned	6
1 Tbsp	Chopped walnuts	1 Tbsp
DRESSING		
1	Garlic clove, crushed	1
¼ tsp	Paprika	¼ tsp
1 Tbsp	White wine vinegar	1 Tbsp
3 Tbsp	Olive oil	3 Tbsp
	Salt and black pepper	
¼ tsp	Sugar	¼ tsp

Arrange the eggs, green and red peppers, mushrooms and olives in a serving dish. Sprinkle with walnuts.

In a screw top jar, combine all the ingredients for the dressing and shake briskly. Pour over the salad. Toss well and serve.

POTATO SALAD WITH HERBS

Fresh herbs are an absolute must for this salad. Experiment with different herbs or use your own favourite combinations.

Below: *Egg Salad*;
Opposite page: *Potato Salad with Herbs*

Metric/U.K.		U.S.
¼kg/½lb	Potatoes, cooked, peeled and cubed	½lb
4	Spring onions (scallions), trimmed and chopped	4
2 tsp	Chopped parsley	2 tsp
1 tsp	Chopped fresh basil	1 tsp
½ tsp	Chopped fresh marjoram	½ sp
¼ tsp	Chopped fresh lemon thyme	¼ tsp
¼ tsp	Chopped fresh fennel leaves	¼ tsp
4 Tbsp	French dressing (see page 12)	4 Tbsp

In a mixing bowl, combine potatoes, spring onions (scallions), parsley, basil, marjoram, lemon thyme and fennel. Pour the French dressing over the potato mixture and toss well. Serve at once.

WATERCRESS, FENNEL, CUCUMBER AND TOMATO SALAD

Metric/U.K.		U.S.
½	Bunch watercress, washed and shaken dry	½
¼	Fennel, trimmed and sliced	¼
¼	Small cucumber, thinly sliced	¼
2	Tomatoes, quartered	2
3	Anchovies, halved	3
1	Spring onion (scallion), finely chopped	1
1 Tbs	Chopped pimento	1 Tbs
3 Tbs	French dressing	3 Tbs

Combine all the salad ingredients in a medium salad bowl. Add the dressing mixture and toss until well mixed.

Serve at once.

GREEN PEPPER SALAD

Metric/U.K.		U.S.
½	Medium-sized cucumber, peeled, quartered lengthways and halved	½

1	Medium-sized green pepper, pith removed, seeded and cut into thin slices	1
1	Small onion, thinly sliced and pushed out into rings	1
2 tsp	Lemon juice	2 tsp
	Salt	
150ml/¼ pint	Plain yoghurt	⅔ cup
1 Tbsp	Olive oil	1 Tbsp
1 tsp	White wine vinegar	1 tsp
1 tsp	Sugar	1 tsp
1 Tbsp	Chopped fresh mint	1 Tbsp

Arrange cucumber in a shallow serving dish and top with green pepper and onion. Sprinkle with lemon juice and salt to taste.

In a small bowl, beat the yoghurt with oil, vinegar and sugar. Pour dressing over cucumber mixture and toss well. Sprinkle with mint and serve at once.

ingredients for the dressing and shake briskly. Pour over the beans. Toss well and chill for 30 minutes in the refrigerator before serving.

Tomato, Watercress and Fennel Salad

CUCUMBER AND TOMATO SALAD

Metric/U.K.		U.S.
1	Medium-sized cucumber, peeled, halved and cut into 1·25cm/½ inch lengths	1
	Salt	
2 Tbsp	Olive oil	2 Tbsp
1	Small onion quartered and sliced	1
1	Garlic clove, crushed	1
100g/¼lb	Tomatoes, blanched, peeled and chopped	¼lb
1 Tbsp	Tomato purée (paste)	1 Tbsp
1 Tbsp	Red wine vinegar	1 Tbsp
a pinch	Dried thyme	a pinch
a pinch	Dried basil	a pinch
	Black pepper	

In a large saucepan cover the cucumber with water and add a little salt. Bring to the boil over moderate heat and cook uncovered for 2 minutes. Drain, rinse and dry on absorbent kitchen paper.

In a frying-pan heat the oil and fry the onion and garlic for 5 minutes. Off the heat, stir in tomatoes, tomato purée (paste), vinegar, thyme, basil, pepper and salt to taste. Add cucumber and toss salad well.

Turn into a serving dish, allow to cool then chill in the refrigerator for 1½ hours before serving.

MELON SALAD

Metric/U.K.		U.S.
1	Small Cantaloup melon	1
2	Small tomatoes, blanched, peeled and sliced	2
1	Small green pepper, pith removed, seeded and chopped	1
2	Spring onions (scallions), trimmed and finely chopped	2

FRENCH (GREEN) BEAN SALAD

Metric/U.K.		U.S.
¼kg/½lb	Fresh French (green) beans, trimmed	½lb
	DRESSING	
1 Tbsp	Red wine vinegar	1 Tbsp
3 Tbsp	Olive oil	3 Tbsp
	Salt and black pepper	
¼ tsp	French mustard	¼ tsp
1 tsp	Chopped fresh dill	1 tsp
1 tsp	Chopped parsley	1 tsp
1	Garlic clove, crushed	1

Cook the beans in simmering salted water for 5 to 15 minutes, depending on size and quality. The beans should be crisp but not limp. Drain, rinse under cold water and place in a large bowl.

In a screw top jar, combine all the

	Mayonnaise (see page	
2 Tbsp	12)	2 Tbsp
1 Tbsp	Sour cream	1 Tbsp
a pinch	Ground ginger	a pinch

Cut a slice from the bottom of the melon so it will stand firm. Cut a 2.5 cm/1 inch slice from the top and scoop out and discard seeds. Scoop out flesh and cut into 2.5 cm/1 inch cubes.

Combine melon cubes and the remaining ingredients and spoon into the melon shell. Chill in the refrigerator for 1 hour before serving.

RAITA

A refreshing but piquant salad to serve with kebabs (see pages 88 and 89). If you don't

Raita (Indian Yoghurt Salad)

want such a fiery taste, remove the seeds from the chilli pod before chopping.

Metric/U.K.		U.S.
300ml/½ pint	Plain yoghurt	1¼ cups
	Medium sized cucumber, diced and	
¼	dégorged	¼
	Spring onions	
	(scallions), trimmed	
2	and finely chopped	2
	Salt and black pepper	
	Fresh green chilli,	
1	finely chopped	1
a pinch	Paprika	a pinch

In a mixing bowl, beat the yoghurt until it is smooth. Stir in cucumber, spring onions (scallions), salt and pepper.

Pour yoghurt mixture into a serving bowl and chill in the refrigerator, covered, for 1 hour.

Before serving, sprinkle over chilli and paprika.

ORANGE AND CARROT SALAD

Metric/U.K.		U.S.
1	Large orange	1
	Carrots, scraped and	
¼kg/½lb	grated	½lb
2 Tbsp	Lemon juice	2 Tbsp
	Salt	
½ tsp	Sugar	½ tsp

Cut the orange in half and squeeze out the juice into a bowl. Scoop out and discard flesh in shells and set shells aside.

Stir carrot into the orange juice and stir in lemon juice, salt and sugar. Chill in the refrigerator for 2 hours.

When ready to serve, spoon carrot mixture into shells and serve at once.

SHALLOT AND MUSHROOM SALAD

Metric/U.K.		U.S.
1	Garlic clove, halved	1
	Small button mushrooms wiped	
¼kg/½lb	clean	2 cups
1 tsp	Lemon juice	1 tsp
	French dressing (see	
100ml/4floz	page 12)	½ cup
	Shallots, blanched, peeled and finely	
2	chopped	2
	Chopped fresh	
2 tsp	marjoram	2 tsp

Rub 2 individual serving bowls with the

garlic, and discard the garlic. Divide the mushrooms between the bowls and sprinkle with lemon juice.

Combine the French dressing, shallots and marjoram. Pour over mushrooms and toss well. Leave at room temperature for 1 hour before serving.

RADISH, CELERY AND CUCUMBER SALAD

Metric/U.K.		U.S.
175g/6oz	Radishes, trimmed	6oz
	Celery stalks,	
3	chopped	3
$\frac{1}{3}$	Small cucumber, diced	$\frac{1}{3}$
50g/2oz	Cashew nuts	$\frac{1}{3}$ cup
a pinch	Dried chervil	a pinch
a pinch	Dried tarragon	a pinch
	Salt and black pepper	
75ml/3floz	Sour cream	$\frac{1}{3}$ cup
	Mayonnaise (see page	
2 tsp	12)	2 tsp
2 tsp	Cider vinegar	2 tsp

Combine the radishes, celery, cucumber, nuts, chervil and tarragon in a serving dish.

In a small bowl, beat together the salt,

Stuffed Apple Salad

pepper, sour cream, mayonnaise and vinegar. Pour dressing over vegetables and toss well.

Serve at once, or chill until required.

STUFFED APPLE SALAD

Metric/U.K.		U.S.
	Large green dessert	
2	apples, cored	2
1 tsp	Lemon juice	1 tsp
	Celery stalks,	
2	chopped	2
	Small green pepper,	
	pith removed, seeded	
$\frac{1}{2}$	and chopped	$\frac{1}{2}$
	Small seedless orange,	
	peeled, pith removed	
$\frac{1}{2}$	and segmented	$\frac{1}{2}$
1 tsp	Celery salt	1 tsp
	Black pepper	
a pinch	Cayenne pepper	a pinch
100ml/4floz	Plain yoghurt	$\frac{1}{2}$ cup
	Grapes, peeled,	
4	halved and seeded	4

Cut a 1cm/$\frac{1}{2}$ inch slice from the stalk end of each apple. Scoop out the flesh with a

74

small melon baler, leaving a 6mm/¼ inch shell. Sprinkle the insides of the shells with half the lemon juice. Reserve half the apple balls and keep the rest for another dish.

Put the apple balls in a bowl and sprinkle with remaining lemon juice. Add celery, green pepper, orange, celery salt, pepper and cayenne and mix well. Stir in yoghurt.

Divide filling between apple shells and garnish with grapes. Chill in the refrigerator for 15 minutes before serving.

PEAR SALAD

This salad will also make a refreshing appetizer.

Metric/U.K.		U.S.
1 Tbsp	Cream cheese	1 Tbsp
1 Tbsp	Single (light) cream	1 Tbsp
1 Tbsp	Lemon juice	1 Tbsp
2 tsp	Apricot jam, strained	2 tsp
	Mayonnaise (see page	
5 Tbsp	12)	5 Tbsp
	Small lettuce,	
1	separated into leaves	1
	Large, ripe pears,	
	peeled, cored and	
2	sliced	2
2 tsp	Capers	2 tsp

In a small bowl, mash the cheese, cream, lemon juice and jam together. Beat in mayonnaise.

Arrange lettuce leaves on individual plates. Arrange the pear slices on top and pour over the dressing. Sprinkle with capers and serve at once.

Pear Salad

DANISH BLUE SALAD

Metric/U.K.		U.S.
	Danish blue cheese,	
50g/2oz	crumbled	½ cup
50g/2oz	Cheddar cheese, diced	2oz
	Small red pepper, pith	
	removed, seeded and	
1	thinly sliced	1
	Spring onions	
	(scallions), trimmed	
3	and finely chopped	3
2 tsp	Fresh chopped dill	2 tsp
DRESSING		
½ tsp	French mustard	½ tsp
3 Tbsp	Olive oil	3 Tbsp
1 Tbsp	White wine vinegar	1 Tbsp
¼ tsp	Paprika	¼ tsp
	Salt and black pepper	

In a screw top jar, combine all the ingredients for the dressing and shake briskly.

Sweetcorn Salad

Metric/U.K.		U.S.
	Salt and black pepper	
a pinch	Tabasco sauce	a pinch
½ tsp	Dry mustard	½ tsp
1	Garlic clove, crushed	1

Place sweetcorn, green pepper, pimento and spring onions (scallions) in a salad bowl and mix well.

Put the dressing ingredients in a screw top jar and shake briskly. Pour the dressing over the sweetcorn mixture and toss well to mix.

Leave at room temperature for 2 hours. Remove and discard bay leaf before serving.

CARROT AND RADISH SALAD

A recipe from Japan. The Japanese white radish (daikon) is best, but the red-skinned variety may be used instead.

Metric/U.K.		U.S.
100g/¼lb	Carrots, scraped and cut into thin strips	¼lb
175g/6oz	White radishes, peeled and cut into thin strips	6oz
1 tsp	Salt	1 tsp
DRESSING		
50ml/2floz	Cider vinegar	¼ cup
2 tsp	Sugar	2 tsp
1 tsp	Soy sauce	1 tsp
6mm/¼in piece	Fresh root ginger, peeled and chopped	¼in piece

Place the carrots and radishes in a bowl and sprinkle with salt. Set aside for 45 minutes. Drain off the water that appears and dry on absorbent kitchen paper. Place carrots and radishes in a salad bowl.

Put all the dressing ingredients in a screw top jar and shake briskly. Pour dressing over vegetables, toss gently and serve.

TOMATO AND FRENCH (GREEN) BEAN SALAD

Metric/U.K.		U.S.
100g/¼lb	Tomatoes, thinly sliced	¼lb
	French (green) beans, trimmed, cooked	

Combine the cheeses, red pepper, spring onions (scallions) and dill in a salad bowl. Pour over dressing and toss well. Serve at once.

SWEETCORN SALAD

Metric/U.K.		U.S.
¼kg/½lb	Canned sweetcorn, drained	½lb
½	Small green pepper, pith removed, seeded and chopped	½
1	Canned pimento, drained and chopped	1
2	Spring onions (scallions), trimmed and chopped	2
DRESSING		
2 Tbsp	Olive oil	2 Tbsp
2 tsp	White wine vinegar	2 tsp
1	Bayleaf	1
1 tsp	Soft (light) brown sugar	1 tsp

Metric/U.K.		U.S.
100g/¼lb	and drained	¼lb
	French dressing (see	
3 Tbsp	page 12)	3 Tbsp

Arrange tomatoes and French (green) beans in a serving dish and pour over the French dressing.

Toss the salad well. Chill in the refrigerator for 15 minutes before serving.

CAULIFLOWER SALAD

If you don't have any Roquefort cheese, any type of blue cheese may be substituted with success.

Metric/U.K.		U.S.
	Small cauliflower,	
	broken into small	
1	florets	1
25g/1oz	Walnuts, chopped	¼ cup
DRESSING		
3 Tbsp	Olive oil	3 Tbsp
1 Tbsp	White wine vinegar	1 Tbsp
½ tsp	Lemon juice	½ tsp
¼ tsp	French mustard	¼ tsp
¼ tsp	Sugar	¼ tsp
	Salt and black pepper	
2 tsp	Chopped parsley	2 tsp
	Roquefort cheese,	
1 Tbsp	finely crumbled	1 Tbsp

Place cauliflower and walnuts into a salad bowl, mix and set aside. Put all the dressing ingredients in a screw top jar and shake briskly. Pour dressing over cauliflower and toss well.

Chill in the refrigerator for 30 minutes before serving.

OLIVE AND SWEETCORN SALAD

Metric/U.K.		U.S.
	Canned sweetcorn,	
175g/6oz	drained	6oz

Tomato and French (Green) Bean Salad

2	Celery stalks, chopped	2
75ml/3floz	Sour cream	⅓ cup
	Salt and black pepper	
¼ tsp	French mustard	¼ tsp
¼ tsp	Sugar	¼ tsp
6	Green stuffed olives	6
1	Small lettuce, separated into leaves	1

Combine the sweetcorn and celery in a bowl and set aside. Beat the sour cream, salt, pepper, mustard and sugar together until smooth.

Slice half the olives and add to the sour cream mixture. Pour dressing over sweetcorn and celery and toss well.

Line a salad bowl with lettuce leaves and spoon mixture into bowl. Garnish with remaining olives. Chill in the refrigerator for 30 minutes before serving.

Wilted Lettuce Salad

WILTED LETTUCE SALAD

An undeservedly derogatory name for this delicious salad.

Metric/U.K.		U.S.
1	Small lettuce	1
	Streaky (fatty) bacon slices, rinds removed	
3	and chopped	3
2 Tbsp	White wine vinegar	2 Tbsp
½ tsp	Sugar	½ tsp
	Black pepper	
	Spring onions (scallions), trimmed	
3	and chopped	3

Tear the lettuce leaves into shreds and place in a salad bowl.

Fry the bacon in a frying-pan over

moderate heat for 5 minutes or until crisp, scraping pan to prevent sticking. Drain on absorbent kitchen paper.

Stir vinegar, sugar, pepper and spring onions (scallions) into fat in the pan and bring to the boil. Pour mixture over the lettuce.

Toss well, sprinkle with bacon and serve.

LETTUCE HEART AND FRUIT SALAD

Blanching the green pepper makes it more digestible.

Metric/U.K.		U.S.
1	Lettuce heart, halved	1
	Small grapefruit, peeled, pith removed	
1	and segmented	1
	Large orange, peeled pith removed and	
1	segmented	1
	Small green pepper, blanched, pith removed,	
1	seeded and sliced	1
2 tsp	Capers	2 tsp
	French dressing (see	
3 Tbsp	page 12)	3 Tbsp

Arrange the lettuce on 2 individual plates and top with grapefruit, orange and green pepper. Sprinkle with capers. Chill in the refrigerator for 1 hour. Spoon over the dressing, and serve.

WATERCRESS, ORANGE AND OLIVE SALAD

Metric/U.K.		U.S.
1	Small bunch watercress	1
	Large orange, peeled, pith removed and	
1	segmented	1
	Black olives, stoned	
2	(pitted) and chopped	2
DRESSING		
1 Tbsp	Fresh orange juice	1 Tbsp
1 tsp	Grated orange zest	1 tsp
2 Tbsp	Orange marmalade	2 Tbsp
	Salt and black pepper	
3 Tbsp	Olive oil	3 Tbsp

Put all the dressing ingredients in a screw top jar and shake briskly.

Arrange the watercress and orange decoratively on a serving plate. Sprinkle with olives. Dribble the dressing over the salad until it is completely covered. Serve at once.

Salad Niçoise

SALAD NIÇOISE

An excellent way to use up any leftover cooked potatoes and beans. A crisp lettuce such as Webb's or Iceberg is ideal for this salad.

Metric/U.K.		U.S.
	Cold, cooked French	
175g/6oz	(green) beans	6oz
	Medium-sized cold cooked potatoes, peeled	
3	and diced	3
	Tomatoes, blanched	
3	peeled and quartered	3
	French dressing (see	
50ml/2floz	page 12)	¼ cup
1	Lettuce heart	1

6	Anchovy fillets, halved	6
10	Black olives	10
1 Tbsp	Capers	1 Tbsp

Cut the beans into 2.5cm/1 inch lengths and place in a large bowl. Add the potatoes and tomatoes. Pour over French dressing and toss well.

Pull the lettuce heart apart and arrange leaves on a serving plate. Pile dressed ingredients on to lettuce. Garnish with anchovy fillets, olives and capers. Serve at once.

PINEAPPLE AND LETTUCE SALAD

Metric/U.K.		U.S.
1	Small pineapple, peeled cored and sliced	1
1	Lettuce heart, torn into shreds	1
2 tsp	Capers	2 tsp
2	Watercress sprigs	2
DRESSING		
3 Tbsp	Sour cream	3 Tbsp
1 Tbsp	Mayonnaise (see page 12)	1 Tbsp
1 tsp	Lemon juice	1 tsp
1 tsp	Light rum (optional)	1 tsp
	Salt and black pepper	
small		small
pinch	Sugar	pinch
2 tsp	Chopped fresh chives	2 tsp

Halve 1 of the pineapple slices and set aside. Chop the remainder into small pieces and place in a bowl with the lettuce and capers.

In a small bowl, beat all the dressing ingredients together until well combined. Pour over pineapple mixture and toss well.

Arrange salad on 2 plates, garnish with the reserved pineapple and watercress. Serve at once.

PEAR AND CHICORY (FRENCH OR BELGIAN ENDIVE) SALAD

Metric/U.K.		U.S.
100g/¼lb	Chicory, (French or Belgian endive) trimmed and sliced	¼lb
1	Large, ripe pear, peeled, cored and sliced	1
1 Tbsp	Walnuts, chopped	1 Tbsp
1 Tbsp	Seedless raisins	1 Tbsp
4	Lettuce leaves	4
DRESSING		
3 Tbsp	Olive oil	3 Tbsp
1 Tbsp	White wine vinegar	1 Tbsp
	Salt and black pepper	
½ tsp	French mustard	½ tsp
½ tsp	Sugar	½ tsp

Place chicory (endive), pear, walnuts and raisins in a bowl. Put all the dressing ingredients in a screw top jar and shake briskly. Pour over salad in bowl and toss well.

Line 2 plates with the lettuce leaves. Spoon salad on top and serve at once.

MIMOSA SALAD

Metric/U.K.		U.S.
1	Lettuce heart, shredded	1
¼	Bunch watercress chopped	¼
1	Celery stalk, chopped	1
1½ Tbsp	French dressing (see page 12)	1½ Tbsp
1	Hard-boiled (hard-cooked) egg yolk, chopped	1
GARNISH		
1	Orange, peeled, pith removed and segmented	1
1 tsp	Olive oil	1 tsp
½ tsp	White wine vinegar	½ tsp
1	Small banana, thinly sliced	1
2 tsp	Lemon juice	2 tsp
5	Green seedless grapes, halved	5
2tsp	Single (light) cream	2 tsp

In a salad bowl, combine lettuce, watercress, celery, French dressing and egg yolk. Toss well to coat with dressing.

In a small bowl combine orange, oil and vinegar. In another small bowl, combine banana and lemon juice and in a third bowl combine the grapes and cream.

Arrange the fruits and their dressings decoratively over the top of the salad. Serve at once.

GREEN SALAD

Metric/U.K.		U.S.
1	Small lettuce, separated into leaves	1
1	Small head chicory, trimmed and separated into leaves	1
1	Small bunch watercress	1
4 Tbsp	French dressing (see page 12)	4 Tbsp

Place lettuce, chicory and watercress in a serving bowl and mix well. Pour over French dressing and toss. Serve at once.

MAIN COURSE MEALS

BRAISED BEEF ROUND

This recipe will serve about 4 people. For 2 people, eat it hot on one day and then use the rest of the meat in another recipe.

Metric/U.K.		U.S.
	Lean topside or silver	
1kg/2lb	side, in one piece	2lb
25g/1oz	Flour	¼ cup
25g/1oz	Butter	2 Tbsp
2	Small onions, sliced	2
1	Garlic clove, crushed	1
	Medium-sized carrots,	
2	scraped and chopped	2
	Small turnip, peeled	
½	and diced	½
	Small head fennel,	
½	sliced	½
	Streaky (fatty) bacon	
2	slices	2
150ml/¼ pint	Dry red wine	⅔ cup
150ml/¼ pint	Beef stock	⅔ cup
	Salt and black pepper	
1	Bay leaf	1
½ tsp	Dried thyme	½ tsp
	Large potato, peeled and	
1	diced	1

Preheat the oven to 170°C/325°F (gas mark 3). Reserve 1 tablespoon of the flour and use the remainder to coat the beef. Melt the butter in a large flameproof casserole and fry the meat on all sides until completely browned. Remove from casserole and set aside.

Add half the onions, garlic, half the carrots, turnip and fennel. Cook for 5 minutes, stirring. Pour vegetables and pan juices into a small bowl. Place the bacon in the bottom of the casserole. Arrange cooked vegetables and pour over juices. Put meat on top of vegetables. Pour over wine and stock, and add salt, pepper, bay leaf and thyme. Bring to the boil and cover tightly.

Cook in centre of the oven for 3 hours.

Remove meat from casserole and set aside. Strain liquid, pressing vegetables to extract juices. Discard contents of strainer and return strained liquid to casserole. Replace meat and add remaining carrots and onions and the potato. Cover and cook in the oven for 45 minutes.

Transfer meat to warmed serving dish and arrange vegetables around it.

Sprinkle the reserved flour into the liquid in the casserole and cook over moderate heat, stirring, for 1 minute until thickened. Pour into a sauce boat and serve at once, poured over the meat.

STEAKS WITH CRUSHED PEPPERCORNS

The brandy and cream may be omitted if preferred, and the steaks just served with the pan juices poured over.

Metric/U.K.		U.S.
2	Entrecôte steaks	2
	Salt	
	Black peppercorns,	
1½ Tbsp	crushed	1½ Tbsp
25g/1oz	Butter	2 Tbsp
1 Tbsp	Brandy	1 Tbsp
75ml/3floz	Double (heavy) cream	⅓ cup

Rub the steaks all over with salt. Press crushed peppercorns into steaks and shake off any excess.

In a large frying-pan melt the butter over moderately high heat, and fry steaks for 2 minutes on each side. Reduce heat to low and cook for a further 2 minutes on each side. This produces rare steaks; double the time if you prefer them well-done.

Transfer steaks to a serving dish and keep hot. Add brandy to pan and stir in cream. Cook for about 2 minutes, stirring constantly.

Pour the sauce over steaks and serve at once.

ESSEX MEAT LAYER PUDDING

Metric/U.K.		U.S.
15g/½oz	Butter	1 Tbsp
1	Medium-sized onion, finely chopped	1
¼kg/½lb	Minced (ground) beef	½lb
½ tsp	Dried oregano	½ tsp
	Salt and black pepper	
a pinch	Celery salt	a pinch
½ Tbsp	Flour	½ Tbsp
½ Tbsp	Very finely chopped fresh chives	½ Tbsp
1	Egg yolk	1
1 Tbsp	Double (heavy) cream	1 Tbsp
SUET PASTRY		
100g/¼lb	Flour	1 cup
small		small
pinch	Salt	pinch
50g/2oz	Shredded suet	½ cup
4 Tbsp	Cold water	4 Tbsp

Essex Meat Layer Pudding

First make the pastry. Sift flour and salt into a bowl. Using your fingers, rub in the suet until thoroughly combined. Add just enough water to make a stiff dough. Form dough into a ball, wrap in greaseproof (waxed) paper and chill in the refrigerator while you make the filling.

In a large frying-pan melt the butter and

fry the onion for 5 minutes until soft. Add beef, oregano, salt, pepper, celery salt and flour to the pan. Stir and cook for 5 minutes. Stir in chives and remove pan from heat.

Beat the egg yolk and cream together, then stir into meat mixture. Cook for a further 5 minutes, stirring from time to time. Remove pan from heat.

Grease a 900ml/1½ pint (1 quart) pudding basin. On a lightly floured surface, roll the pastry out to 6mm/¼ inch thick. Cut out a small circle of pastry to fit the bottom of the basin. Place in the basin and top with a layer – about 2.5cm/1 inch thick – of the filling. Continue making layers, finishing with a layer of pastry. The filling will not fill the basin completely as extra space is needed for rising during steaming.

Cut out a circle of greaseproof (waxed) paper and one of foil 10cm/4 inches larger than the diameter of the basin. Grease the paper and place on top of the foil, greased side away from foil. Holding them together, make a 2.5cm/1 inch pleat across the centre. Place, foil uppermost, over the pudding basin and tie with string, leaving a loop for lifting the basin.

Place basin in a large saucepan and pour in enough boiling water to come two-thirds of the way up the sides. Cover and steam over low heat for 3 hours. Add more boiling water if water level drops.

Remove foil and paper circles. Put a plate over the top of the basin and invert pudding on to plate. Serve at once.

MEAT LOAF

Metric/U.K.		U.S.
¼kg/½lb	Minced (ground) beef	½ lb
40g/1½oz	Fresh breadcrumbs	¾ cup
1	Small onion, finely chopped	1
50g/2oz	Mushrooms, wiped clean and chopped	½ cup
1	Egg, lightly beaten	1
1 tsp	French mustard	1 tsp
½ tsp	Celery salt	½ tsp
1 tsp	Worcestershire sauce	1 tsp
	Black pepper	
¼ tsp	Dried marjoram	¼ tsp
1 Tbsp	Chopped parsley	1 Tbsp
a pinch	Dried thyme	a pinch
2	Streaky (fatty) bacon slices	2

Preheat the oven to 170°C/325°F (gas mark 3).

In a large bowl, combine all the in-

Meatballs American Style

84

gredients except the bacon. Mix and knead well. Press meat mixture into a ½kg/1lb loaf tin, smooth the top and lay bacon on top.

Put tin into a large baking tin half-filled with boiling water. Bake in the centre of the oven for 1½ hours.

Pour off any fat and leave to cool for 1 hour. Run a knife round the edges and turn out on to a plate. Wrap meat loaf in foil and chill in the refrigerator for 4 hours before serving.

MEATBALLS AMERICAN-STYLE

The secret of making these meatballs smooth is by kneading them for longer time than usual.

Metric/U.K.		U.S.
	Thin slices white bread,	
2	crusts removed	2
350g/¾lb	Minced (ground) beef	¾lb
	Small onion, very finely	
1	chopped	1
	Small egg, lightly	
1	beaten	1
50ml/2floz	Tomato ketchup	¼ cup
	Salt and black pepper	
1½ Tbsp	Water	1½ Tbsp
TOMATO SAUCE		
1 Tbsp	Vegetable oil	1 Tbsp
	Small onion, finely	
1	chopped	1
	Canned peeled tomatoes	
200g/7oz	with their can juice	7oz
2 Tbsp	Tomato purée (paste)	2 Tbsp
	Chicken stock (bouillon)	
½	cube, crumbled	½
½ Tbsp	Worcestershire sauce	½ Tbsp
	Salt and black pepper	
	Gravy browning	
1 tsp	dissolved	1 tsp
1 Tbsp	in water	1 Tbsp

Soak bread in cold water for 5 minutes. Squeeze to extract water and place in a large bowl. Add beef, onion, egg, tomato ketchup, salt and pepper. Knead the mixture for 5 minutes until very smooth. Add the water and knead for a further 5 minutes. Shape the mixture into small balls and place in the refrigerator while you make the sauce.

In a large saucepan, heat the oil and fry

onion for 5 minutes until soft. Stir in tomatoes, their can juice, tomato purée (paste), stock cube, Worcestershire sauce, salt, pepper and gravy browning. Bringing to the boil, cover, reduce the heat to low and simmer for 20 minutes.

Drop the meatballs into the sauce, and cook gently, shaking the pan from time to time, for 30 minutes. Serve at once.

Chilli Con Carne

CHILLI CON CARNE

Metric/U.K.		U.S.
2 tsp	Olive oil	2 tsp
	Small onion, finely	
1	sliced	1
1	Garlic clove, crushed	1
¼kg/½lb	Minced (ground) beef	½lb
	Canned peeled tomatoes	
200g/7oz	with their can juice	7oz
2 Tbsp	Tomato purée (paste)	2 Tbsp
1	Bay leaf	1
½ tsp	Ground cumin	½ tsp
½ tsp	Dried oregano	½ tsp
¼ tsp	Cayenne pepper	¼ tsp
2 tsp	Mild chilli powder	2 tsp
	Salt	
100ml/4floz	Beef stock	½ cup
	Canned red kidney	
200g/7oz	beans, drained	7oz

In a large saucepan, heat the oil and fry onion and garlic for 5 minutes until soft.

Stir in meat and cook for 2 minutes, stirring. Add tomatoes, their can juice, tomato purée (paste), bay leaf, cumin, oregano, cayenne, chilli powder, salt and stock. Cover the pan and bring to the boil over moderate heat. Reduce heat to low and simmer for 1 hour.

Add kidney beans, cover and simmer for 30 minutes. Remove bay leaf and serve at once.

CARBONNADE OF BEEF

Metric/U.K.		U.S.
25g/1oz	Seasoned flour	¼ cup
	Braising steak, cut into	
½kg/1lb	2.5cm/1 inch cubes	1lb
2 Tbsp	Vegetable oil	2 Tbsp
	Medium-sized onions,	
3	thinly sliced	3
1	Garlic clove, crushed	1
300ml/½ pint	Canned or bottled beer	1¼ cups
2 tsp	Soft (light) brown sugar	2 tsp
1	Bouquet garni	1

Place seasoned flour on a large plate and roll the meat in flour until well coated.

Heat the oil in a flameproof casserole over moderate heat. Fry meat until browned. Remove meat from pan and add onions and garlic. Fry for 10 minutes until onions are soft. Return meat to pan and add beer, sugar and bouquet garni..

Cover the casserole, reduce heat to low and simmer for 2 hours.

If there is too much liquid, uncover the pan and bring to the boil. Boil until liquid reduces. Remove and discard bouquet garni and serve.

HAMBURGERS

Other accompaniments to serve with this sublime American invention are pickles, relishes, ketchup, mayonnaise and French mustard.

Metric/U.K.		U.S.
½kg/1lb	Minced (ground) beef	1lb
15g/½oz	Fresh breadcrumbs	¼ cup
	Salt and black pepper	
¼ tsp	Dried thyme	¼ tsp
	Small egg, lightly	
1	beaten	1
	Buttered hamburger or	
2	large soft buns, warmed	2
ACCOMPANIMENTS		
	Large tomato, thinly	
1	sliced	1
	Small onion, sliced and	
½	pushed out into rings	½
2	Lettuce leaves	2

In a bowl, combine the beef, breadcrumbs, salt, pepper, thyme and egg. Form into 2 balls and flatten into patty shapes. Grill (broil) under high heat for 2 to 3 minutes on each side. Reduce heat and grill (broil)

for a further 5 minutes on each side.

Place a hamburger in each bun and top with tomato, onion and lettuce. Serve at once.

STUFFED BEEF ROLLS

Metric/U.K.		U.S.
	Thin lean beef slices, each 13cm/5 inch square	
4		4
1 Tbsp	Vegetable oil	1 Tbsp
1	Onion, chopped	1
1	Carrot, scraped and diced	1
150ml/¼ pint	Beef stock	⅔ cup
100g/¼lb	Tomatoes, blanched, peeled and sliced	¼lb
1	Garlic clove, crushed	1
1	Bay leaf	1
1 Tbsp	Chopped parsley	1 Tbsp
STUFFING		
75g/3oz	Minced (ground) beef or pork	3oz
1	Small onion, finely chopped	1

87

Metric/U.K.		U.S.
15g/½oz	Softened butter	1 Tbsp
	Fresh white	
15g/½oz	breadcrumbs	¼ cup
2 tsp	Chopped parsley	2 tsp
½ tsp	Dried sage	½ tsp
2 tsp	Grated lemon zest	2 tsp
	Small egg, lightly	
1	beaten	1
	Green stuffed olives,	
3	chopped	3
	Salt and black pepper	

Preheat the oven to 180°C/350°F (gas mark 4). Combine all the stuffing ingredients and mix well. Lay the beef slices out flat, spread with stuffing and roll up. Secure with string.

Heat the oil in a flameproof casserole and fry the beef rolls until browned all over. Remove from pan. Add onion and carrot and cook for 3 minutes, stirring. Add stock, tomatoes, garlic and bay leaf. Lay beef rolls on top and cover. Cook in the oven for 1½ hours.

Remove beef rolls from casserole, remove string and arrange on a serving plate. Keep hot. Strain the liquid, pressing vegetables to extract juices. Discard contents of strainer. Pour strained juices over beef rolls and serve at once, sprinkled with parsley.

Duch Beef Pancake (Crêpe)

DUTCH BEEF PANCAKE (CRÊPE)

Make up the basic pancake (crêpe) batter and make 2 thick pancakes (crêpes) instead of the 8 thin ones.

Metric/U.K.		U.S.
15g/½oz	Butter	1 Tbsp
	Medium-sized onion,	
1	finely chopped	1
350g/¾lb	Minced (ground) beef	¾lb
	Mushrooms, wiped	
50g/2oz	clean and sliced	½ cup
75ml/3floz	Double (heavy) cream	⅓ cup
	Salt and black pepper	
1 Tbsp	Chopped parsley	1 Tbsp
	Thick pancakes	
	(crêpes) made with	
	savoury pancake	
	(crêpe) batter (see page	
2	12), kept hot	2

In a large frying-pan, melt the butter and fry the onion for 5 minutes until soft. Add beef and fry for 5 minutes, stirring. Add mushrooms and fry for 3 minutes. Remove as much liquid as possible with a spoon or bulb baster. Stir in cream, salt, pepper and parsley. Cover, reduce heat to low and simmer for 20 minutes, stirring from time to time.

Place 1 pancake (crêpe) on a large serving plate. Spread meat filling over and top with other pancake (crêpe). Cut in half and serve at once.

GREEK LAMB KEBABS

The weight of the meat is calculated after boning. Leg of lamb may be used instead of shoulder.

Metric/U.K.		U.S.
2 Tbsp	Lemon juice	2 Tbsp
4 Tbsp	Olive oil	4 Tbsp
	Salt and black pepper	
¼ tsp	Dried marjoram	¼ tsp
	Boned shoulder of lamb,	
	cut into 2.5cm/1 inch	
½kg/1lb	cubes	1lb
	Large onion, quartered	
	and separated into	
1	layers	1

Mix the lemon juice, olive oil, salt, pepper and marjoram together in a shallow dish. Add the meat and toss well. Cover and marinate at room temperature for 1 hour, turning lamb from time to time.

Remove lamb from marinade. Thread lamb on to skewers alternately with the onion. Discard marinade.

Cook kebabs under a hot grill (broiler) for 8 minutes, turning to brown all sides. Reduce heat to moderate and cook for a further 8 minutes, turning or until cooked. Serve at once.

KEBABS MARINATED IN YOGHURT

If the kebabs are to be served with rice, ease meat and vegetables off the skewers on to rice and pour the cooking juices from the grill (broiler) pan over the top.

Metric/U.K.		U.S.
75ml/3floz	Plain yoghurt	⅓ cup
½ tsp	Fresh rosemary	½ tsp
1	Garlic clove, crushed	1
	Salt and black pepper	
½kg/1lb	Boned leg of lamb, cut into 2.5cm/1 inch cubes	1lb
1	Small red or green pepper, pith removed, seeded and cut into pieces	1
2	Small onions, cut into quarters	2

Greek Lamb Kebabs

Mix the yoghurt, rosemary, garlic, salt and pepper together in a shallow dish. Add lamb and toss to coat in the mixture. Cover and marinate at room temperature for 5 hours or overnight in the refrigerator, turning lamb from time to time.

Remove lamb from marinade. Thread lamb on to skewers, alternating with pepper and onion. Discard marinade.

Cook kebabs under a hot grill (broiler) for 8 minutes, turning to brown all sides. Reduce heat to moderate and cook for a further 8 minutes, turning.

Serve at once.

MUSTARD-BASTED LAMB

The flavour of the meat after cooking is gentle but incredibly tasty. Shoulder of lamb has a higher proportion of fat and bone than other cuts, but the meat is sweet and succulent. Again, use any leftover meat for another dish. Make gravy with the water any accompanying green vegetables are cooked in.

Metric/U.K.		U.S.
1kg/2lb	Half lamb shoulder	2lb
	Salt	
1	Garlic clove, crushed	1
2 Tbsp	French mustard	2 Tbsp
½ tsp	Ground ginger	½ tsp
2 tsp	Soy sauce	2 tsp
1 Tbsp	Olive oil	1 Tbsp

Skin the lamb and wipe with a damp cloth. Rub salt into the fat. Combine garlic, mustard, ginger, soy sauce and olive oil. Place lamb on a rack in a roasting tin, brush with the mustard mixture and leave in a cool place for 3 hours.

Preheat the oven to 180°C/350°F (gas mark 4). Roast lamb for 1½ hours, turning twice during cooking. Transfer lamb to a serving plate and keep hot while you make the gravy. Serve at once.

Lamb Patties Greek Style

LAMB PATTIES GREEK-STYLE

Pine nuts would make these delicious little patties more authentic, but almonds can be used.

Metric/U.K.		U.S.
½kg/1lb	Minced (ground) lamb	1lb
½	Small onion, grated	½
	Salt and black pepper	
¼ tsp	Grated nutmeg	¼ tsp
	Blanched almonds,	
50g/2oz	roughly chopped	½ cup

In a large bowl combine all the ingredients, mixing well with your hands until well blended. Flour your hands and form the mixture into 6 small patties.

Cook the patties under a hot grill (broiler) for 8 minutes on each side or until cooked through. If the patties brown too quickly, reduce heat to moderate after the first 2 minutes. Serve at once.

LEG OF LAMB WITH CORIANDER AND GARLIC

Here is a recipe which gives you the luxury flavour of a large piece of meat. It is expensive, but the leftover lamb can be made into numerous other meals thus balancing your housekeeping books.

Metric/U.K.		U.S.
2.5kg/5lb	Leg of lamb	5lb
4	Garlic cloves, halved	4
1 Tbsp	Crushed coriander seeds	1 Tbsp
	Salt and black pepper	
25g/1oz	Butter	2 Tbsp

Preheat the oven to 190°C/375°F (gas mark 5).

Use the point of a sharp knife to make 8 incisions in the lamb, near to the bone. Push the garlic and coriander into the incisions. Rub lamb all over with salt and pepper, place in a roasting tin and dot with butter.

Roast for 2 hours; this will produce medium-rare meat. If you prefer the meat

well done, reduce the heat to 170°C/325°F (gas mark 3) and continue cooking for a further 30 minutes.

If you are serving the meat hot, carve into thick slices. To serve cold, leave the meat to cool completely before carving.

MOUSSAKA

This is a basic version of the traditional Greek dish. If you can find it, use the Greek kefalotiri cheese, instead of the Parmesan substituted here.

Metric/U.K.		U.S.
15g/½oz	Butter	1 Tbsp
1	Small onion, finely chopped	1
1	Garlic clove, crushed	1
¼kg/½lb	Minced (ground) lamb	½lb
2	Medium-sized skinned tomatoes, coarsely chopped	2
1 Tbsp	Tomato purée (paste)	1 Tbsp
¼ tsp	Dried thyme	¼ tsp
	Salt and black pepper	
¼kg/½lb	Aubergines (eggplants), sliced and dégorged	½lb
1½ Tbsp	Flour	1½ Tbsp
50ml/2floz	Vegetable oil	¼ cup
225ml/½ pint	Béchamel sauce (see page 13)	1¼ cups
1	Egg yolk	1
2 Tbsp	Grated Parmesan cheese	2 Tbsp

Moussaka

Preheat the oven to 190°C/375°F (gas mark 5).

In a frying-pan melt the butter and fry the onion and garlic over moderate heat for 5 minutes until soft. Add meat and cook for 5 minutes, stirring. Add tomatoes, tomato purée (paste), thyme, salt and pepper and cook for further 3 minutes, stirring. Remove from heat and set aside.

Rinse aubergines (eggplants) and pat dry on absorbent kitchen paper. Dip in flour, shaking off excess. Heat the oil in a large frying-pan and fry aubergine (eggplant) slices for 3 minutes on each side, adding more oil if necessary. Drain on absorbent kitchen paper.

Arrange half the aubergine (eggplant) slices in the bottom of an ovenproof dish.

91

Spoon over lamb mixture and top with remaining aubergine (eggplant) slices.

Beat together the béchamel sauce and egg yolk and spread over the aubergine (eggplant) slices. Sprinkle with cheese and bake for 35 minutes. Serve at once.

LAMB CHOPS WITH ROSEMARY

Metric/U.K.		U.S.
2 Tbsp	Olive oil	2 Tbsp
1 Tbsp	Lemon juice	1 Tbsp
	Salt and black pepper	
1 tsp	Dried rosemary	1 tsp
1	Garlic clove, crushed	1
2	Thick lamb chops	2

Combine the oil, lemon juice, salt, pepper, rosemary and garlic in a shallow dish. Place lamb chops in the marinade and baste well. Set aside in a cool place to marinate for 2 hours, basting from time to time.

Remove chops from marinade. Cook chops under a hot grill (broiler) for 2 minutes on each side. Reduce the heat to moderately low and grill (broil) for a further 8 minutes on each side basting from time to time, with marinade, or until tender.

Arrange the chops on a serving plate, spoon over the pan juices and serve at once.

LANCASHIRE HOT POT

The traditional recipe, using lamb cutlets, kidneys and oysters. However, because of their cost, the oysters may be omitted.

Metric/U.K.		U.S.
350g/¾lb	Potatoes, peeled and thickly sliced	¾ lb
	Salt	
4	Lamb cutlets, trimmed of excess fat	4
100g/¼lb	Mushrooms, wiped clean and sliced	1 cup
2	Lamb's kidneys, fat, skin and core removed, and sliced	2
1	Small onion, sliced	1
	Black pepper	
½ tsp	Dried thyme	½ tsp
6	Fresh oysters, shelled	6
150ml/¼ pint	Beef stock, thickened with gravy browning	⅔ cup
1 tsp		1 tsp

Preheat the oven to 180°C/350°F (gas mark 4).

Lancashire Hot Pot

Cover the bottom of a deep ovenproof casserole with half the potatoes, and sprinkle with salt. Arrange cutlets on top of potatoes and cover with mushrooms, kidneys and onion. Sprinkle with more salt, pepper and thyme. Cover with oysters and remaining potatoes. Pour in thickened stock. Cover and cook in the oven for 2 hours. Remove lid, increase heat to 200°C/400°F (gas mark 6) and cook for 30 minutes to brown potatoes. Serve at once.

PEPPERS STUFFED WITH LAMB AND RICE

Metric/U.K.		U.S.
2	Large red peppers	2
2 tsp	Vegetable oil	2 tsp
½	Small onion, finely chopped	½
1	Small garlic clove, crushed	1
100g/¼lb	Minced (ground) lamb	¼lb
200g/7oz	Canned peeled tomatoes with their can juice	7oz
	Salt and black pepper	
½ tsp	Coriander seeds, crushed	½ tsp
50g/2oz	Cooked long-grain rice	⅓ cup
¼ tsp	Dried mint	¼ tsp

Remove the stalks, and cut a 2.5 cm/1 inch slice from the wider end of each pepper. Remove pith and seeds from insides of peppers and set aside. Preheat the oven to 190°C/375°F (gas mark 5).

Heat the oil over moderate heat and fry the onion and garlic for 3 minutes or until soft. Add lamb and cook for 5 minutes until browned. Add tomatoes, their can juice, salt, pepper and coriander. Cover, reduce heat to low and simmer for 20 minutes. Add rice and mint and cook for a further 5 minutes. Remove from heat.

Spoon filling into peppers and place in a greased ovenproof dish. Cook in centre of the oven for 40 minutes. Serve at once.

STUFFED BREAST OF LAMB

Metric/U.K.		U.S.
1	Large lean breast of lamb, boned	1
1 Tbsp	Vegetable oil	1 Tbsp

Stuffed Breast of Lamb

Metric/U.K.		U.S.
100g/¼lb	Dried apricots, soaked overnight in water	⅔ cup
1 Tbsp	Sugar	1 Tbsp
STUFFING		
1 Tbsp	Vegetable oil	1 Tbsp
1	Small onion, finely chopped	1
100g/¼lb	Minced (ground) beef or sausage meat	¼lb
1 Tbsp	Long-grain rice	1 Tbsp
½ tsp	Ground cumin	½ tsp
6 Tbsp	Water	6 Tbsp
1½ Tbsp	Chopped parsley	1½ Tbsp
	Salt and black pepper	
2 Tbsp	Chopped almond	2 Tbsp
2 Tbsp	Seedless raisins	2 Tbsp

First make the stuffing. Heat the oil over moderate heat and fry onion for 5 minutes until soft. Add meat and cook for 5 minutes until browned. Stir in rice, cumin, water, parsley, salt and pepper. Bring to the boil, cover, reduce the heat to low and simmer for 25 minutes. Remove from heat and, stir in almonds and raisins.

Preheat the oven to 180°C/350°F (gas mark 4). Spread stuffing over lamb, roll up and secure with string. Place in a roasting tin, brush with oil, and roast for 2 hours.

Meanwhile, prepare apricots. Place apricots, their soaking water and sugar in a small pan and bring to the boil. Reduce heat to low and simmer for 30 minutes until pulpy.

When lamb is cooked, pour off cooking liquids in the roasting tin. Increase oven temperature to 230°C/450°F (gas mark 8). Pour apricot mixture over lamb and roast for 10 minutes. Serve at once.

BARBECUED PORK SPARE-RIBS

Metric/U.K.		U.S.
1 Tbsp	Vegetable oil	1 Tbsp
1	Garlic clove, crushed	1
1	Small onion, finely chopped	1
5 Tbsp	Tomato purée (paste)	5 Tbsp
1½ Tbsp	Lemon juice	1½ Tbsp
	Salt and black pepper	
¼ tsp	Dried sage	¼ tsp
2 Tbsp	Soft (light) brown sugar	2 Tbsp
4 Tbsp	Beef stock	4 Tbsp
2 Tbsp	Worcestershire sauce	2 Tbsp
1 tsp	Dry mustard	1 tsp
¾kg/1½lb	Pork spare-ribs, chopped into serving pieces	1½lb

Preheat the oven to 200°C/400°F (gas mark 6).
Heat the oil in a frying-pan over moderate heat and fry the garlic and onion for 5 minutes. Add tomato purée (paste), lemon

Barbecued Spare-Ribs

juice, salt, pepper, sage, sugar, stock, Worcestershire sauce and mustard and stir well. Reduce heat to low and simmer for 5 minutes, stirring.

Put spare-ribs on a rack in a large roasting tin. Pour over sauce and bake for 1 hour, basting frequently. Serve very hot.

PORK CHOPS WITH MUSHROOMS AND PARSLEY STUFFING

Some butchers sell these very thick chops under the name of double loin pork chops.

Metric/U.K.		U.S.
2	Thick loin pork chops	2
½ Tbsp	Chopped parsley	½ Tbsp
15g/½oz	Fresh white breadcrumbs	¼ cup
a pinch	Cayenne pepper	a pinch
	Salt and black pepper	
15g/½oz	Butter	1 Tbsp
½	Small onion, finely chopped	½
1	Small garlic clove, crushed	1
25g/1oz	Mushrooms, wiped clean and finely chopped	¼ cup
½ Tbsp	Vegetable oil	½ Tbsp
25g/1oz	Maître d'Hôtel butter, sliced (see page 13)	2 Tbsp

Preheat the oven to 170°C/325°F (gas mark 3). Use a sharp knife to cut horizontal slits in the meatiest part of the chops to make pockets.

Combine the parsley, breadcrumbs, cayenne, salt and pepper. Set aside. In a small saucepan, melt the butter and fry the onion and garlic for 3 minutes until soft. Add mushrooms and cook for 2 minutes, stirring. Off the heat stir in parsley mixture.

Spoon stuffing into chops and secure with wooden cocktail sticks (toothpicks). Place in a large ovenproof casserole, brush with oil, cover and bake for 1 hour. Remove lid and cook for a further 30 minutes. Place chops on a serving plate, remove sticks (picks), top with maître d'hôtel butter and serve.

SAGE PORK FILLET

Pork fillet (tenderloin) is a relatively expensive

cut, but there is absolutely no wastage as the meat has no bones or fat.

Metric/U.K.		U.S.
½kg/1lb	Pork fillet (tenderloin), in one piece	1lb
	Salt and black pepper	
25g/1oz	Butter	2 Tbsp
1 Tbsp	Fresh chopped sage	1 Tbsp
100g/¼lb	Emmenthal cheese, cut into 6 slices	¼lb
1 Tbsp	French mustard	1 Tbsp
75ml/3floz	Single (light) cream	⅛ cup

Rub pork all over with salt and pepper and set aside. In a flameproof casserole, melt the butter and add sage. Fry the pork over moderate heat for 6 minutes, until browned all over. Reduce heat to low, cover and cook for 40 minutes, turning the meat from time to time.

Remove pork from casserole and place on a chopping board. Make 6 deep incisions along the meat. Spread the cheese slices with three-quarters of the mustard and place 1 slice in each incision. Return pork to casserole and cook uncovered for 5 minutes or until cheese has melted. Transfer to serving plate and keep hot while you make the sauce.

Stir the remaining mustard into the juices in the casserole. Pour in cream, stirring constantly, and cook for 1 minute. Do not boil. Pour into a sauceboat and serve at once, with the meat.

Pork Chops with Mushrooms and Parsley Stuffing

CRISPY ROAST PORK

An adaptation of a Chinese recipe. Five-spice powder can be found at most oriental provision stores. If you use mixed spice instead, take note of the larger amount needed.

Metric/U.K.		U.S.
¾kg/1½lb	Belly of pork	1½lb
	Salt	
½ tsp	Five-spice powder *or*	½ tsp
½ Tbsp	mixed spice	½ Tbsp
2 tsp	Cornflour (cornstarch)	2 tsp
	mixed to a paste with	
1	small egg white	1
2 Tbsp	Soy sauce	2 Tbsp
2 Tbsp	Tomato ketchup	2 Tbsp

Rub the pork all over with salt and spice powder or mixed spice. Set aside in a cool place (not the refrigerator) overnight.

Preheat the oven to 190°C/375°F (gas mark 5). Quickly dip pork in boiling water —the meat should be in the water only for a second or two. Dry with absorbent kitchen paper. Rub pork all over with cornflour (cornstarch) mixture.

Roast on a rack in a roasting tin for 1¼ hours. Reduce oven temperature if the meat looks too browned. Remove pork from oven and place on a carving board. Cut into 6 mm/¼ inch thick slices.

Mix together the soy sauce and tomato ketchup, and serve at once, with the pork.

SHREDDED PORK STIR-FRIED WITH SPRING GREENS

Metric/U.K.		U.S.
175g/6oz	Lean pork, cut into strips	6oz
	Salt and black pepper	
1 tsp	Cornflour (cornstarch)	1 tsp
1½ Tbsp	Vegetable oil	1½ Tbsp
¼kg/½lb	Spring greens or green cabbage, shredded	½lb
2 tsp	Butter	2 tsp
2 Tbsp	Beef stock	2 Tbsp
1 Tbsp	Soy sauce	1 Tbsp
½ tsp	Sugar	½ tsp
1 Tbsp	Dry sherry	1 Tbsp

Place pork strips on a board and rub in the salt, pepper and cornflour (cornstarch).

Heat the oil in a large frying-pan and fry the pork for 3 minutes, over moderate heat, stirring constantly. Push pork to one side of the pan and add the greens or cabbage with the butter. Stir to mix. Reduce heat to moderate and stir in stock, soy sauce and sugar. Fry, turning constantly, for 3 minutes.

Stir pork into vegetables to mix well. Pour over sherry and fry for a further 1 minute. Serve at once.

LOIN OF PORK WITH GARLIC AND VEGETABLES

Metric/U.K.		U.S.
1½kg/3lb	Boned loin of pork, trimmed of excess fat and rolled	3lb
	Salt and black pepper	
6	Garlic cloves	6
50g/2oz	Butter	¼ cup
2	Medium-sized onions, sliced and pushed out into rings	2
1	Small head celery, cut into 1·25cm/½ inch lengths	1
300ml/½ pint	Chicken stock	1¼ cups
4	Medium-sized potatoes, peeled and sliced	4
4	Medium-sized tomatoes, blanched, peeled and chopped	4
1 tsp	Dried thyme	1 tsp
150ml/¼ pint	Sour cream	⅔ cup

Rub pork all over with salt and pepper. Use the point of a sharp knife to make incisions in the meat. Slice 4 of the garlic cloves and insert these into the incisions.

Melt the butter in a large flameproof casserole and fry the meat over moderate heat for 10 minutes, turning to brown all over. Remove meat and set aside.

Add onions and celery and cook for 5 minutes. Stir in stock, potatoes, tomatoes, thyme and the 2 whole garlic cloves. Bring to the boil, reduce heat to low, add pork and cover. Cook for 2½ hours.

Transfer meat to a serving plate and carve into thick slices. Keep hot while you make the sauce. Strain the liquid into a small pan, rubbing vegetables through strainer. Discard contents of strainer. Stir sour cream into strained liquid, and cook over low heat

until smooth. Pour sauce into a sauceboat and serve at once, with the meat.

PORK AND APPLE CASSEROLE

Sometimes called hand and spring of pork, this cut is cheaper but just as tasty as the more expensive joints. The meat is weighed after boning.

Metric/U.K.		U.S.
½kg/1lb	Boned hand of pork	1lb
	Medium-sized onion,	
1	chopped	1
2 tsp	Fresh chopped sage	2 tsp
	Salt and black pepper	
	Large tart dessert apple,	
1	peeled, cored and sliced	1
125ml/4floz	Water or dry cider	½ cup
½kg/1lb	Potatoes, peeled	1lb
1 Tbsp	Hot milk	1 Tbsp
	Butter	

Remove any excess fat from the pork and cut into cubes. Place half the pork in a flameproof casserole. Cover with onion, sage, salt and pepper, then apple. Add remaining pork and water or cider. Bring to the boil, reduce heat to very low, cover and simmer for 2 hours.

About 30 minutes before the end of the cooking time, boil and mash the potatoes with milk and butter. When pork is cooked, cover with mashed potato and dot with more butter. Cook under a hot grill (broiler) for 10 minutes, or until potato is browned on top. Serve at once.

PORK AND BEAN STEW

Metric/U.K.		U.S.
	Dried white haricot	
	(navy) beans, soaked	
175g/6oz	overnight and drained	1 cup
600ml/1 pint	Water	2½ cups
2 Tbsp	Olive oil	2 Tbsp
	Lean pork, cut into	
350g/¾lb	5cm/2 inch cubes	¾lb
	Small carrot, scraped	
1	and sliced	1
	Small turnip, peeled	
½	and quartered	½
1	Small onion, sliced	1
1	Garlic clove, crushed	1
	Salt and black pepper	
½ tsp	Paprika	½ tsp
½ tsp	Dried basil	½ tsp
50g/2oz	Tomato purée (paste)	¼ cup
175ml/6floz	Chicken stock	¾ cup

Put the beans and water in a large pan and bring to the boil. Reduce heat to moderate and simmer, covered, for 1 hour. Drain, return beans to pan and set aside.

Heat the oil and fry the pork over moderate heat for 5 minutes. Add carrot, turnip, onion, garlic, salt, pepper, paprika and basil. Cook for 3 minutes, stirring. Add pork mixture to beans in pan. Stir in tomato purée (paste) and stock. Bring to the boil, reduce heat to low, cover and simmer for 2½ hours. Serve at once.

Metric/U.K.		U.S.
1½ Tbsp	Flour	1½ Tbsp
1 Tbsp	Lemon juice	1 Tbsp
	Salt and white pepper	
1	Egg yolk	1
2 Tbsp	Double (heavy) cream	2 Tbsp
2 tsp	Capers	2 tsp

Combine egg, breadcrumbs, anchovy extract, salt and pepper. Set aside for 15 minutes. Melt the butter and fry the onion over moderate heat for 5 minutes. Add pork and fry for a further 5 minutes. Allow to cool slightly then add to the breadcrumb mixture. Knead until stiff. With floured hands, shape mixture into balls and chill in the refrigerator for 30 minutes.

Bring the stock to the boil in a large saucepan. Add meatballs, reduce heat to low and simmer for 25 minutes. Arrange meatballs on a serving plate and keep hot. Strain the stock, return to high heat and reduce to 300 ml/½ pint (1¼ cups). Remove from heat and set aside.

To make the sauce, melt the butter and fry the onion for 3 minutes. Stir in the flour and cook for 1 minute. Off the heat gradually stir in the stock, then the lemon juice, salt and pepper. Beat in the egg yolk and cream and capers. Heat gently but do not boil. Pour sauce over meatballs and serve at once.

OSSO BUCCO

A classic Italian stew made with veal knuckle or shank. The meat (the cut is called osso bucco) is sold on the bone and sawn into pieces; enthusiasts consider the best part is scraping out the marrow from the middle of the bone. The gremolata (or gremolada) is a subtle flavouring component and is added at the end of the cooking time.

PORK MEATBALLS IN LEMON AND CAPER SAUCE

Metric/U.K.		U.S.
1	Egg	1
25g/1oz	Fresh white breadcrumbs	½ cup
1 tsp	Anchovy extract	1 tsp
	Salt and black pepper	
10g/¼oz	Butter	½ Tbsp
1	Small onion, very finely chopped	1
½kg/1lb	Minced (ground) pork	1lb
900ml/1½ pints	Beef stock	3¾ cups
SAUCE		
15g/½oz	Butter	1 Tbsp
½	Small onion, very finely chopped	½

Metric/U.K.		U.S.
25g/1oz	Seasoned flour	¼ cup
1kg/2lb	Veal knuckle or shank, sawn into 8cm/3 inch pieces	2lb
40g/1½oz	Butter	3 Tbsp
1	Small onion, thinly sliced	1
200g/7oz	Canned peeled tomatoes with their can juice	7oz
2 tsp	Tomato purée (paste)	2 tsp
150ml/¼ pint	Dry white wine	⅔ cup

	Salt and black pepper	
½ tsp	Sugar	½ tsp
GREMOLATA		
2 tsp	Finely grated lemon zest	2 tsp
1	Garlic clove, crushed	1
1 Tbsp	Chopped parsley	1 Tbsp

Place seasoned flour on a plate and coat veal in the flour, shaking off any excess.

In a large flameproof casserole, melt the butter and fry the veal over moderate heat for 5 minutes, turning to brown all over. Remove from casserole. Add onion and fry for 5 minutes until soft. Add tomatoes, their can juice, and the tomato purée (paste) and cook for 2 minutes. Stir in wine, salt, pepper and sugar. Add veal, bring to the boil, reduce heat to low, cover and simmer for 2 hours. Mix all the gremolata ingredients together and stir into the casserole. Cook for 1 minute. Serve at once.

VEAL ESCALOPES (SCALLOPINI) WITH HAM AND CHEESE

Metric/U.K.		U.S.
2	Thin slices cooked ham	2
2	Thin slices Gruyère cheese	2
4	Small veal escalopes (scallopini), pounded thin	4
	Black pepper	
¼ tsp	Dried marjoram	¼ tsp
2 Tbsp	Flour	2 Tbsp
1	Egg, beaten	1
25g/1oz	Dry white breadcrumbs	¼ cup
50g/2oz	Butter	¼ cup
4	Lemon slices	4

Place a slice of ham and a slice of cheese on 2 of the escalopes (scallopini). Cover with remaining 2 to make 'sandwiches'. Pound the edges to seal. Sprinkle with pepper and marjoram, then dip in flour.

Dip escalopes (scallopini) in egg and breadcrumbs, coating them thoroughly. Wrap in greaseproof (waxed) paper and chill in the refrigerator for 30 minutes.

In a large frying-pan melt the butter and fry the escalopes (scallopini) over moderate heat for 3 minutes on each side. Reduce heat to low and cook for a further 8 minutes on each side. Arrange on a serving plate, garnish with lemon and serve at once.

Above: *Veal Escalopes (Scallopini) with Ham and Cheese;* Opposite: *Osso Buco*

ROAST CHICKEN WITH APRICOTS

Metric/U.K.		U.S.
25g/1oz	Butter	2 Tbsp
½	Small onion, finely chopped	½
100g/¼lb	Pork sausage meat	¼lb
2 Tbsp	Fresh white breadcrumbs	2 Tbsp
1 Tbsp	Single (light) cream	1 Tbsp
	Salt and black pepper	
¼ tsp	Dried thyme	¼ tsp
½ tsp	Dried marjoram	½ tsp
2 tsp	Hazelnuts or almonds, finely chopped	2 tsp
¼kg/½lb	Canned apricot halves, finely chopped, with	½lb
4 Tbsp	can juice reserved	4 Tbsp
1½kg/3lb	Chicken	3lb
½ Tbsp	Soft (light) brown sugar	½ Tbsp
150ml/¼ pint	Chicken stock or white wine	⅔ cup
1	Garlic clove, crushed	1

In a saucepan, melt half the butter and fry the onion over moderate heat for 3 minutes. Add sausage meat and cook, stirring, for 5 minutes. Stir in breadcrumbs, cream, salt, pepper, thyme, marjoram, nuts and 1 tablespoon of chopped apricots. Cook, stirring for 2 minutes. Remove pan from heat and set aside.

Preheat oven to 220°C/425°F (gas mark 7). Rub chicken all over with more salt and pepper. Spoon stuffing into chicken and secure opening with thread or skewers.

Place chicken in a roasting tin and roast for 15 minutes.

Meanwhile, in a small saucepan, combine remaining apricots, reserved can juice, sugar, stock or wine, garlic and remaining butter. Bring to the boil over moderate heat, reduce heat to low and cook, stirring, for 5 minutes. Strain the mixture, rubbing apricots through strainer. Discard contents of strainer. Reduce oven temperature to 180°C/350°F (gas mark 4), spoon sauce over chicken and roast for a further 1½ hours, basting frequently.

Carve chicken into serving pieces. Skim off any fat on the surface of sauce and serve at once, with the chicken.

MARYLAND CHICKEN

Recipes for this famous dish vary tremendously. Traditional accompaniments include corn fritters, fried, bananas, bacon rolls, potato pancakes (crêpes), boiled rice and horseradish sauce.

Maryland Chicken

Metric/U.K.		U.S.
175ml/6floz	Milk	¾ cup
2 Tbsp	Seasoned flour	2 Tbsp
	Chicken breasts, skinned	
2	and boned	2
1	Small egg, beaten	1
	Fresh white	
40g/1½oz	breadcrumbs	¾ cup
50g/2oz	Butter	¼ cup
1½ Tbsp	Vegetable oil	1½ Tbsp
½ tsp	Sugar	½ tsp
2 tsp	Flour	2 tsp

Pour 2 Tbsp of the milk in a saucer. Dip the chicken in milk, then flour, shaking off any excess flour. Set aside for 10 minutes to allow coating to dry slightly.

Dip chicken in egg and breadcrumbs, shaking off any excess. Melt 40 g/1½ oz (3 Tbsp) of the butter in a frying-pan and fry the chicken over low heat for 20 minutes, turning to cook both sides. Drain chicken on absorbent kitchen paper and keep hot.

Melt the remaining butter in a small saucepan and stir in sugar. Stir over moderate heat until sugar caramelizes and darkens. Stir in flour and cook for 1 minute. Off the heat gradually stir in remaining milk. Cook for 2 minutes until sauce is smooth. Pour into a sauceboat and serve at once, with the chicken.

PEANUT BUTTER AND CHICKEN STEW

Metric/U.K.		U.S.
1 Tbsp	Peanut or vegetable oil	1 Tbsp
1	Small onion, chopped	1
1	Garlic clove, crushed	1
	Small green pepper, pith removed, seeded and	
1	chopped	1
2	Chicken pieces	2
100g/¼lb	Peanut butter	½ cup
300ml/½ pint	Chicken stock	1¼ cups
	Salt and black pepper	
½ tsp	Turmeric	½ tsp
2 tsp	Ground coriander	2 tsp
½ tsp	Ground cumin	½ tsp
¼ tsp	Hot chilli powder	¼ tsp
2	Tomatoes, blanched, peeled and chopped	2
2 tsp	Chopped parsley	2 tsp

Heat the oil in a saucepan and fry the onion, garlic and green pepper for 5 minutes over moderate heat, until onion is soft. Add chicken and fry for 8 minutes, turning to brown both sides.

Meanwhile, combine peanut butter, 4 tablespoons stock, salt, pepper, turmeric, coriander, cumin and chilli powder, and mix to a smooth paste. Stir paste into pan and cook, stirring constantly, for 5 minutes. Pour in remaining stock and add tomatoes. Reduce heat to low, cover and simmer for 1 hour. Uncover the pan for the last 15 minutes of cooking time. Transfer the stew to a serving dish and serve at once, sprinkled with parsley.

YOGHURT CHICKEN

Metric/U.K.		U.S.
1½kg/3lb	Chicken, skinned	3lb
	Salt	
2 Tbsp	Lemon juice	2 Tbsp
	Fresh green chilli, very	
1	finely chopped	1
150ml/¼ pint	Plain yoghurt	⅔ cup
	Fresh coriander leaves,	
2 Tbsp	finely chopped	2 Tbsp
	Fresh root ginger, peeled	
2.5cm/1in piece	and finely chopped	1in piece

Peanut Butter and Chicken Stew

2	Garlic cloves, crushed	2
2 Tbsp	Butter, melted	2 Tbsp

Prick the chicken all over with a fork, and rub all over with salt, lemon juice and chilli. Place chicken in a large bowl and set aside for 30 minutes. Combine yoghurt, coriander, ginger and garlic and rub all over chicken. Cover the bowl and set aside in a cool place (not the refrigerator) for 8 hours or overnight.

Preheat the oven to 200°C/400°F (gas mark 6). Place chicken in a roasting tin and pour over butter. Roast for 20 minutes, then reduce heat to 180°C/350°F (gas mark 4) and roast for a further 1 hour, basting frequently.

Lift chicken from tin, place on a serving dish and keep hot. Place tin over moderate heat and boil the juices for 3 minutes, stirring constantly, until they have thickened. Pour sauce over chicken and serve at once.

STUFFED CHICKEN DRUMSTICKS

Metric/U.K.		U.S.
	Large chicken	
4	drumsticks, boned	4
4	Cooked slices ham	4
	Canned peach halves,	
2	drained and halved	2
	Salt and black pepper	
40g/1½oz	Butter	3 Tbsp
	Canned condensed	
200ml/7floz	mushroom soup	1 cup
	Chicken stock	
	or	
150ml/¼ pint	dry white wine	⅔ cup

Stuff each drumstick with a slice of ham and a peach quarter. Season and secure openings with wooden cocktail sticks (toothpicks).

Melt the butter in a flameproof casserole and fry the chicken for 5 minutes, turning to

Opposite page: *Yoghurt Chicken;* Below: *Stuffed Chicken Drumsticks*

brown all over. Stir in mushroom soup and wine or stock. Bring to the boil, reduce heat to low, cover and simmer for 1 hour. Serve at once, straight from the casserole.

GRILLED (BROILED) CHICKEN WITH HERBS

You can use any combination of fresh chopped herbs.

Metric/U.K.		U.S.
2	Chicken pieces	2
1	Garlic clove, halved	1
	Salt and black pepper	
50g/2oz	Butter	¼ cup
1 Tbsp	Olive oil	1 Tbsp
1 Tbsp	Lemon juice	1 Tbsp
2 tsp	Chopped parsley	2 tps
2 tsp	Chopped fresh basil	2 tsp

Rub the chicken pieces all over with the garlic, then with salt and pepper. Discard garlic.

In a small saucepan melt the butter with the oil. Remove pan from heat and stir in lemon juice, parsley and basil. Brush the chicken with the butter mixture.

Cook the chicken under a moderately hot grill (broiler) for 10 minutes on each side, basting frequently. Transfer to a serving plate, spoon over juices in the grill (broiler) pan and serve at once.

MOZZARELLA CHICKEN

Metric/U.K.		U.S.
1 Tbsp	Vegetable oil	1 Tbsp
1	Small onion, finely chopped	1
	Canned peeled tomatoes, with their can	
200g/7oz	juice	7oz
1 Tbsp	Tomato purée paste	1 Tbsp
½ tsp	Dried oregano	½ tsp
	Salt and black pepper	
	Streaky (fatty) bacon	
2	slices, rinds removed	2
15g/½oz	Butter	1 Tbsp
a pinch	Dried tarragon	a pinch
2	Chicken breasts, skinned and boned	2
50g/2oz	Mozzarella cheese, cut into slices	½ cup

In a saucepan, heat the oil and fry the onion over moderate heat for 5 minutes until soft. Add tomatoes, their can juice, tomato purée (paste), oregano, salt and pepper. Stir, bring to the boil, reduce heat to low, cover and simmer for 20 minutes.

Meanwhile fry the bacon in a frying-pan over moderate heat for 5 minutes until crisp. Drain on absorbent kitchen paper and keep hot. Add butter to pan and stir in tarragon. Fry chicken for 15 minutes, over low heat, turning to cook both sides. Transfer chicken to a flameproof serving dish, top each with a slice of bacon and pour over sauce. Place cheese slices on top and place under a hot grill (broiler) for 5 minutes to melt cheese. Serve at once.

CHICKEN AND LEEK PIE

Metric/U.K.		U.S.
3	Chicken pieces	3
1	Small onion, halved	1
1	Celery stalk, chopped	1
1	Bouquet garni	1
	Salt	
300ml/½ pint	Water	1¼ cups
	Leeks, including 5cm/2 inches of green	
½kg/1lb	stem, sliced	1lb
	Cooked ham, thinly	
50g/2oz	sliced	2oz
2 tsp	Chopped parsley	2 tsp
	Shortcrust pastry (see	
100g/¼lb	page 13)	¼lb
1	Small egg, beaten	1
	Single (light) cream,	
2 Tbsp	warmed (optional)	2 Tbsp

Place chicken, onion, celery, bouquet garni and salt in a large saucepan and pour in water. Bring to the boil and skim off any scum which rises to the surface. Reduce heat to low, partly cover and simmer for 1 hour.

Transfer chicken to a board, skin and remove meat from bones. Cut meat into bite-sized pieces and place in a small pie dish. Set aside.

Strain stock, pressing vegetables to extract juices. Discard contents of strainer. Return 150ml/¼ pint (⅔ cup) of the stock to the saucepan, add leeks and bring to the boil. Reduce heat to low, cover and simmer leeks for 15 minutes.

Preheat the oven to 200°C/400°F (gas

mark 6). Pour the leeks and stock into the pie dish. Arrange ham over the top, leaving a small gap in the middle, and sprinkle with parsley. Roll out the pastry on a floured surface, to 2.5cm/1 inch larger than the top of the pie dish. Cut a 1·25cm/½ inch strip around the pastry, dampen the rim of the dish with water and press the pastry strip on the rim. Dampen the strip and lift the dough on to the dish. Trim and crimp the edges to seal. Cut a cross in the middle of the pastry. Roll out any trimmings and use to decorate pie. Brush pastry with beaten egg. Bake for 45 minutes. Check after 30 minutes, and turn oven down slightly if pastry is browning too quickly.

Pour the warmed cream into the hole in the pastry and serve at once.

POUSSIN WITH BUTTER AND LEMON

A poussin is a small young chicken and neatly serves one. It is served split in half; to do this, push a sharp knife through the breastbone.

Poussin with Butter and Lemon

Take poussin in both hands and bend back until ribs crack. Cut through skin to separate completely.

Metric/U.K.		U.S.
	Poussin, split through	
2	breastbone	2
	Salt and black pepper	
40g/1½oz	Butter	3 Tbsp
2 tsp	Vegetable oil	2 tsp
	Chicken stock or	
4 Tbsp	white wine	4 Tbsp
1 Tbsp	Lemon juice	1 Tbsp
150ml/¼ pint	Single (light) cream	⅔ cup
GARNISH		
1	Lemon, cut into wedges	1
2 tsp	Chopped parsley	2 tsp

Rub poussin all over with salt and pepper. Melt the butter with the oil and fry the poussin halves over moderate heat for 4 minutes on each side. Reduce heat to low, cover and cook for 30 minutes. Transfer to a serving plate and keep hot.

Increase heat to moderate and stir in

stock or wine, lemon juice and cream. Cook the sauce for 2 minutes, stirring. Do not boil.

Pour sauce over poussin and serve at once, garnished with lemon wedges and sprinkled with parsley.

CHICKEN CASSEROLE

Metric/U.K.		U.S.
1 Tbsp	Seasoned flour	1 Tbsp
½ tsp	Dried dill	½ tsp
2	Chicken pieces, skinned	2
1	Small egg, beaten	1
15g/½oz	Butter	1 Tbsp
1 Tbsp	Vegetable oil	1 Tbsp
150ml/¼ pint	Chicken stock	⅔ cup
1	Small green pepper, pith removed, seeded and sliced into rings	1
2	Tomatoes, blanched, peeled and chopped	2
4 Tbsp	Single (light) cream	4 Tbsp
50g/2oz	Cheddar cheese, grated	½ cup

Combine seasoned flour and dill. Dip chicken pieces in egg then flour, shaking off any excess flour.

In a saucepan, melt the butter with the oil and fry the chicken over moderate heat for 8 minutes, turning to brown all over. Add stock and bring to the boil. Reduce heat to low, cover and simmer for 1 hour.

Remove chicken from pan and arrange on a flameproof serving dish. Keep hot.

Add green pepper to liquid in the pan and simmer for 5 minutes. Add tomatoes and simmer for a further 2 minutes. Remove vegetables from pan and arrange around chicken. Stir cream into pan and cook gently for 2 minutes.

Pour sauce over chicken, sprinkle with cheese and place under a hot grill (broiler) for 5 minutes to melt the cheese. Serve at once.

PINEAPPLE AND TURKEY SALAD

Metric/U.K.		U.S.
1	Medium-sized pineapple	1
350g/¾lb	Cooked turkey meat, diced	¾lb

Chicken Casserole

Glamorgan Sausages

2	Celery stalks, diced	2	
1	Small banana, sliced	1	
1 Tbsp	Salted peanuts	1 Tbsp	
75ml/3floz	Mayonnaise (see page 12)	⅓ cup	
2 Tbsp	Double (heavy) cream	2 Tbsp	
2 tsp	Apricot jam	2 tsp	
½ tsp	Curry powder	½ tsp	
Salt and black pepper			
GARNISH			
1 Tbsp	Desiccated (shredded) coconut	1 Tbsp	
1	Small orange, peeled, pith removed and sliced	1	

Leaving the green top on, cut the pineapple in half lengthways, scoop out the flesh and cut half the flesh into cubes. Use the rest for another dish. Dry the pineapple shells thoroughly, wrap in foil and chill in the refrigerator for 1 hour.

In a large mixing bowl, combine the chopped pineapple flesh, turkey, celery, banana and peanuts. In a small mixing bowl, mix together mayonnaise, cream, jam, curry powder, salt and pepper. Pour dressing over turkey mixture and toss well.

Spoon turkey mixture into the pineapple shells, garnish with coconut and orange slices and serve at once.

GLAMORGAN SAUSAGES

Metric/U.K.		U.S.
1	Small onion, finely chopped	1
25g/1oz	Cooked ham, finely chopped	1oz
75g/3oz	Cheddar cheese, grated	¾ cup
50g/2oz	Fresh white breadcrumbs	1 cup
1 Tbsp	Chopped parsley	1 Tbsp
½ tsp	Dried thyme	½ tsp
	Salt and black pepper	
¼ tsp	Dry mustard	¼ tsp
1	Egg yolk	1
2 Tbsp	Flour	2 Tbsp
1	Egg white, lightly beaten	1
75g/3oz	Dry white breadcrumbs	¾ cup
50g/2oz	Butter	¼ cup
2 Tbsp	Vegetable oil	2 Tbsp

In a mixing bowl, combine the onion, ham, cheese, fresh breadcrumbs, parsley, thyme, salt, pepper, mustard and egg yolk. Mix thoroughly and with floured hands, shape into 8 sausages. Dip each sausage in flour, then egg white, then dry breadcrumbs.

In a large frying-pan, melt the butter

with the oil and fry the sausages for 5 minutes over moderate heat, turning to brown all over. Serve at once.

TOAD IN THE HOLE

Metric/U.K.		U.S.
15g/½oz	Vegetable fat	1 Tbsp
225g/½lb	Pork sausages	½lb
BATTER		
75g/3oz	Flour	¾ cup
	Salt	
1	Small egg	1
225ml/8floz	Milk	1 cup

Preheat the oven to 220°C/425°F (gas mark 7).

For the batter, sift flour and salt into a mixing bowl. Beat in the egg and enough milk to make a stiff, smooth batter. Leave for 5 minutes, then gradually beat in the remaining milk. Set aside.

Put vegetable fat in a baking dish and place dish in the oven. When the fat has melted, arrange sausages in the dish. Cook sausages in the oven for 10 minutes, turning to brown all over.

Pour batter into the dish, reduce oven

temperatures to 200°C/400°F (gas mark 6) and bake for 30 minutes. Serve at once.

KIDNEY CASSEROLE

Metric/U.K.		U.S.
2 Tbsp	Seasoned flour	2 Tbsp
	Lambs' kidneys, cleaned	
8	prepared and sliced	8
	Streaky (fatty) bacon	
4	slices, chopped	4
15g/½oz	Butter	1 Tbsp
1	Small onion, sliced	1
1	Garlic clove, crushed	1
	Button mushrooms,	
6	sliced	6
	Small green pepper,	
	pith removed, seeded	
1	and sliced	1
2 tsp	Soy sauce	2 tsp
150ml/¼ pint	Beef stock	⅔ cup

Place the seasoned flour on a plate and coat the kidney slices in flour, shaking off any excess. Set aside.

In a flameproof casserole, melt the butter and fry the bacon over moderate heat for 5 minutes. Add onion, garlic and green

Toad in the Hole, a traditional British savoury dish.

Glazed Bacon

pepper and fry for 5 minutes, stirring. Push the vegetables to one side and fry the kidneys for 3 minutes, turning to brown all over. Pour in soy sauce and stock and stir well. Bring to the boil, reduce heat to low, add mushrooms, cover and simmer for 20 minutes. Serve at once.

GLAZED BACON

This is also delicious served cold. Allow to become completely cold before slicing.

Metric/U.K.		U.S.
	Bacon (ham) joint,	
¾kg/1½lb	ready to cook	1½lb
2 tsp	Treacle (molasses)	2 tsp
	Soft (light) brown	
2 Tbsp	sugar	2 Tbsp
2 Tbsp	French mustard	2 Tbsp
2 tsp	Dark rum or water	2 tsp
2 tsp	Fresh orange juice	2 tsp

Place joint in a saucepan, cover with cold water and bring to the boil. Reduce heat to low, cover and simmer for 1 hour.

Preheat the oven to 200°C/400°F (gas mark 6). Remove joint from pan. If joint has not been skinned, remove skin. Place joint on a rack in a roasting tin. Mix all the remaining ingredients together and pour mixture over joint. Roast for 20 minutes, basting frequently.

Transfer to a serving plate, carve into thick slices and serve at once.

BRAISED OXTAIL

Metric/U.K.		U.S.
½kg/1lb	Oxtail	1lb
	Salt and black pepper	
a pinch	Ground allspice	a pinch
25g/1oz	Butter	2 Tbsp
1	Small onion, chopped	1
	Carrots, scraped and	
100g/¼lb	chopped	¼lb
1	Bouquet garni	1
150ml/¼ pint	Beef stock	⅔ cup
150ml/¼ pint	Dry red wine	⅔ cup
1 Tbsp	Tomato purée (paste)	1 Tbsp

Rinse the oxtail, shake dry, divide into joints and remove fat. Rub all over with salt, pepper and allspice.

In a large flameproof casserole, melt the butter and fry the oxtail over moderate heat for 5 minutes, turning to brown all over. Remove oxtail from pan and fry onion and carrots for 5 minutes. Return oxtail to pan and add bouquet garni, stock, wine and tomato purée (paste). Bring to the boil, skim off any scum, cover and reduce heat to low. Simmer for 3 hours.

Remove and discard bouquet garni. Leave the casserole to cool and, when cold, chill in the refrigerator for 8 hours or overnight.

Remove and discard fat that has congealed on the surface. Bring casserole to the boil over moderate heat. Reduce heat to low, cover and simmer for 10 minutes. Transfer oxtail pieces to a serving dish. Keep hot.

Bring liquids in casserole to the boil and boil until reduced by one-third. Pour sauce over oxtail and serve at once.

LIVER IN WHITE WINE

Superbly simple to make and quite stunning to eat.

Metric/U.K.		U.S.
25g/1oz	Seasoned flour	¼ cup
	Calf's liver, cut into	
350g/¾lb	1·25cm/½ inch slices	¾lb
25g/1oz	Butter	2 Tbsp
150ml/¼ pint	Dry white wine	⅔ cup
2 Tbsp	Single (light) cream	2 Tbsp

Place seasoned flour on a plate and coat liver in flour, shaking off any excess.

In a frying-pan melt the butter and fry the liver over moderate heat for 1 minute on each side. Pour in wine, bring to the boil,

Braised Oxtail

reduce heat to low and simmer for 2 minutes. Transfer liver to a serving dish and keep hot.

Stir cream into pan and cook gently, stirring, until hot but not boiling. Pour sauce over liver and serve at once.

LIVER WITH TOMATO SAUCE

Metric/U.K.		U.S.
1 Tbsp	Seasoned flour	1 Tbsp
¼kg/½lb	Lamb's liver, thinly sliced	½lb
10g/¼oz	Butter	½ Tbsp
1 Tbsp	Olive oil	1 Tbsp
2 tsp	Chopped parsley	2 tsp
SAUCE		
1 Tbsp	Olive oil	1 Tbsp
1	Small onion, finely chopped	1
1	Garlic clove, crushed	1
100g/¼lb	Mushrooms, wiped clean and sliced	1 cup
200g/7oz	Canned peeled tomatoes with their can juice	7oz
2 Tbsp	Tomato purée (paste)	2 Tbsp
½ tsp	Dried marjoram	½ tsp
¼ tsp	Dried basil	¼ tsp
¼ tsp	Celery seeds	¼ tsp
	Salt and black pepper	
1	Bay leaf	1

For the sauce, heat the oil and fry the onion and garlic over moderate heat for 5 minutes until soft. Add mushrooms and tomatoes with their can juice, and cook for 3 minutes. Stir in tomato purée (paste), marjoram, basil, celery seeds, salt, pepper and bay leaf. Bring to the boil, reduce heat to low, cover and simmer for 30 minutes.

Meanwhile, place seasoned flour on a plate and coat liver with flour, shaking off any excess. Melt the butter with the oil in a large frying-pan and fry the liver over moderate heat for 5 minutes, turning to cook both sides. Transfer liver to a serving dish and pour over sauce. Remove and discard bay leaf and serve at once.

MACKEREL FILLETS WITH HERBS

If you wish to serve this hot, add the herbs to the stock before reducing. Pour hot stock over mackerel and serve.

Metric/U.K.		U.S.
150ml/¼ pint	Fish stock	⅔ cup
1	Mackerel, skinned, boned and filleted	1
½ tsp	Chopped fresh chervil	½ tsp
1 tsp	Chopped fresh chives	1 tsp
1 tsp	Chopped parsley	1 tsp

FISH CAKES

Metric/U.K.		U.S.
	White fish fillets, cooked, skinned and	
275g/10oz	flaked	10oz
	Potatoes, cooked and	
275g/10oz	mashed	10oz
1 Tbsp	Butter melted	1 Tbsp
2	Eggs	2
1 Tbsp	Flour	1 Tbsp
	Salt	
¼ tsp	Cayenne pepper	¼ tsp
2 Tbsp	Chopped parsley	2 Tbsp
100g/¼lb	Dry white breadcrumbs	1 cup
4 Tbsp	Vegetable oil	4 Tbsp
2	Lemon wedges	2

In a large bowl, combine fish, potatoes, butter, 1 egg, flour, salt, cayenne and parsley. Mix well and chill in the refrigerator for 1 hour.

With floured hands, shape the mixture into 6 balls, then flatten balls into patties. Beat the other egg. Dip patties in egg then roll in breadcrumbs, shaking off any excess.

In a large frying-pan heat the oil and fry the fish cakes over high heat for 4 minutes on each side. Serve at once, garnished with lemon wedges.

FISH KEBABS

Metric/U.K.		U.S.
	Mackerel, skinned,	
2	boned and filleted	2
4	Pickling onions	4
4	Small tomatoes	4
	Button mushrooms,	
4	wiped clean	4
	Small green pepper,	
	pith removed, seeded	
1	and cut into strips	1
2 Tbsp	White wine vinegar	2 Tbsp
2 Tbsp	Olive oil	2 Tbsp
	Salt and black pepper	
½ tsp	Dried oregano	½ tsp

Cut the mackerel fillets into bite-sized pieces. Thread on to skewers, alternating with onions, tomatoes, mushrooms and green pepper.

Combine the vinegar, olive oil, salt, pepper and oregano in a shallow dish. Place kebabs in dish and marinate for

Left: Fish Kebabs

Put the fish stock and mackerel fillets in a saucepan and bring to the boil over moderate heat. Cover, reduce heat to low and simmer for 5 minutes. Transfer fish to a serving dish and set aside.

Return pan to high heat and boil the stock until it has reduced by half. Remove from heat and allow stock to cool. Pour over mackerel and sprinkle with chervil, chives and parsley. Chill in the refrigerator for 2 hours before serving.

2 hours at room temperature, turning and basting from time to time.

Cook kebabs under a hot grill (broiler) for 15 minutes, basting with marinade and turning frequently. Serve at once.

HADDOCK WITH POACHED EGGS

Metric/U.K.		U.S.
25g/1oz	Butter	2 Tbsp
300ml/½ pint	Milk	1¼ cups
	Smoked haddock in	
350g/¾lb	2 pieces	¾lb
1 Tbsp	Cornflour (cornstarch)	1 Tbsp
	Black pepper	
	Eggs, poached and	
2	kept hot	2

Melt the butter in a saucepan over moderate heat. Pour in milk and add haddock. Bring to the boil, reduce heat to low, cover and poach for 5 minutes. Carefully transfer haddock to a serving dish and keep hot.

Beat 2 Tbsp of milk from the pan with cornflour (cornstarch). All cornflour (cornstarch) mixture and pepper to milk in pan, increase heat to moderate and cook sauce, stirring for 2 minutes, until thick and smooth.

Place a poached egg on each piece of haddock, surround haddock with sauce and serve at once.

JIFFY TUNA SURPRISE

Metric/U.K.		U.S.
50g/2oz	Butter	¼ cup
	Large onion, finely	
1	chopped	1
1	Garlic clove, crushed	1
½ tsp	Curry powder	½ tsp

Jiffy Tuna Surprise.

Metric/U.K.		U.S.
200g/7oz	Canned peeled tomatoes with their can juice	7oz
¼kg/½lb	Canned tuna fish, flaked	½lb
1 tsp	Dried basil	1 tsp
2 Tbsp	Seedless raisins	2 Tbsp
	Salt and black pepper	

Melt the butter in a saucepan and fry the onion and garlic for 5 minutes over moderate heat. Stir in curry powder, tomatoes with their can juice, tuna, basil, raisins, salt and pepper.

Bring to the boil, reduce heat to low, cover and simmer for 10 minutes.

Turn into a serving dish and serve.

WHITING STUFFED WITH SHRIMP

Metric/U.K.		U.S.
2	Whiting, heads removed and boned	2
½	Lemon	½
	Salt and black pepper	
40g/1½oz	Butter	3 Tbsp
100g/¼lb	Small button mushrooms, wiped clean and sliced	1 cup
100g/¼lb	Shrimps or prawns, shelled (peeled)	¼lb
2 Tbsp	Chopped parsley	2 Tbsp

Preheat the oven to 180°C/350°F (gas mark 4).

Rinse whiting under cold water, pat dry and squeeze lemon all over fish. Rub, inside and out, with salt and pepper.

Melt 15g/½oz (1Tbsp) of the butter in a frying-pan and fry the mushrooms for 2 minutes. Stir in shrimp or prawns and parsley, and cook for 2 minutes. Stuff mixture into cavities of fish.

Arrange stuffed fish in a baking dish, dot with remaining butter and bake for 25 minutes. Serve at once.

FISH MOULD

Metric/U.K.		U.S.
¼kg/½lb	White fish, cooked, skinned, boned and flaked	½lb
300ml/½ pint	Béchamel sauce (see page 13)	1¼ cups
	Salt and white pepper	
15g/½oz	Gelatine, dissolved in 2 Tbsp water	1 Tbsp
1 Tbsp	Double (heavy) cream	1 Tbsp
2	Tomatoes, sliced	2
1	Egg, hard-boiled (hard-cooked) and sliced	1
DRESSING		
150ml/¼ pint	Mayonnaise (see page 12)	⅔ cup

4 Tbsp	Plain yoghurt	4 Tbsp
	Salt	
	Small onion, finely	
I	chopped	I
I Tbsp	Chopped parsley	I Tbsp
	Pickled cucumber,	
I	finely chopped	I
I Tbsp	Chopped pimento	I Tbsp
I Tbsp	Finely chopped celery	I Tbsp

Purée the fish and béchamel sauce in an electric blender and season with salt and pepper. Stir dissolved gelatine and cream into fish mixture. Turn into a mould and chill in the refrigerator for 3 hours until set.

Mix all the dressing ingredients together.

Run a knife around the edge of the mould then quickly dip the bottom in hot water. Invert mould on to a serving plate. Pour over dressing and surround with tomatoes and egg. Serve at once.

WHITE FISH FONDUE

This makes a festive and easy meal for two. Serve with salad and white wine.

Metric/U.K.		U.S.
¼kg/½lb	Hake fillets, cut into cubes	½lb
¼kg/½lb	Cod fillets, cut into cubes	½lb
	Squid, cleaned, blanched	
	skinned, beaten and cut	
¼kg/½lb	into cubes	½lb
	Large prawns (shrimps),	
	shelled and	
¼kg/½lb	deveined	½lb
150ml/¼ pint	Garlic mayonnaise	⅔ cup
300ml/½ pint	Vegetable oil	1¼ cups

Divide the fish equally between two plates. Pour garlic mayonnaise into a small serving dish.

Heat oil in a saucepan until it reaches 190°C/375°F on a deep-fat thermometer. Transfer oil to a fondue pot and light spirit burner. Carefully place pot over light and cook fish by spearing it with a fondue fork and placing in hot oil.

Serve with mayonnaise sauce.

FISH PIE

This fish pie has a delicious potato and cheese sauce topping. You could give it a pastry topping by covering the pie with 100g/¼lb

shortcrust (see page 13) or puff pastry. Any white fish can be used—cod, haddock and even the humble whiting.

Metric/U.K.		U.S.
25g/1oz	Butter	2 Tbsp
	Small onion, finely	
I	chopped	I
	White fish, skinned,	
	boned and cut into	
½kg/1lb	bite-sized pieces	1lb
	Egg, hard-boiled	
	(hard-cooked) and	
I	sliced	I
	Salt and black pepper	
2 Tbsp	Chopped parsley	2 Tbsp
	Potatoes, cooked and	
½kg/1lb	mashed	1lb
	Cheese sauce (see	
150ml/¼ pint	page 13)	⅔ cup

Preheat the oven to 190°C/375°F (gas mark 5).

Melt the butter in a frying-pan and fry the onion over moderate heat for 5 minutes. Add fish and fry for a further 5 minutes. Remove pan from heat and spoon onion and fish mixture into a greased pie dish. Arrange egg slices over the top and sprinkle with salt, pepper and half the parsley. Spoon mashed potatoes over eggs, smoothing over the top. Pour the cheese sauce over the potatoes. Bake for 20 minutes or until golden on top.

Sprinkle with remaining parsley and serve at once.

LEMON SOLE MEUNIERE

A Dover (Gray) sole may be used instead of the lemon sole.

Metric/U.K.		U.S.
	Large lemon sole,	
I	filleted	I
2 Tbsp	Lemon juice	2 Tbsp
2 Tbsp	Seasoned flour	2 Tbsp
a pinch	Grated nutmeg	a pinch
50g/2oz	Butter	¼ cup
4	Lemon slices	4
2	Parsley sprigs	2

Sprinkle fish with ½ tablespoon of the lemon juice. Set aside for 5 minutes. Place flour on a plate and stir in nutmeg. Coat fish in

flour, shaking off any excess.

Melt half the butter in a frying-pan and fry the fish for 2 minutes on each side over moderate heat. Remove pan from heat and transfer fish to a serving dish. Keep hot.

Wipe pan clean and melt remaining butter and remaining lemon juice over moderate heat. Pour sauce over fish, garnish with lemon slices and parsley and serve at once.

KEDGEREE

Kedgeree was created by Indian cooks during the days of the British empire, to combine the British love of smoked fish and their own culinary traditions. The name evolved from the word kitchri, an Indian dish of rice and lentils, sometimes served with smoked fish.

Right: *Kedgeree*

Metric/U.K.		U.S.
50g/2oz	Butter	¼ cup
	Cooked smoked haddock, skinned, boned and	
175g/6oz	flaked	6oz
175g/6oz	Cooked long-grain rice	2½ cups
	Egg, hard-boiled (hard-cooked) and	
1	finely chopped	1
	Salt and black pepper	
a pinch	Cayenne pepper	a pinch
1 Tbsp	Single (light) cream	1 Tbsp
2 tsp	Chopped parsley	2 tsp

Melt 40g/1½oz (3 Tbsp) of the butter in a frying-pan over moderate heat. Add fish, rice, egg, salt, pepper and cayenne. Stir thoroughly, then stir in cream.

Heat the kedgeree for 5 minutes, stirring. Remove from heat and pile into a serving dish. Sprinkle over parsley and dot with remaining butter. Serve at once.

PLAICE (FLOUNDER) BAKED WITH GARLIC AND TOMATOES

Metric/U.K.		U.S.
50g/2oz	Dry white breadcrumbs	½ cup
1 Tbsp	Chopped parsley	1 Tbsp
1	Garlic clove, crushed	1
	Finely grated lemon	
1 tsp	zest	1 tsp
	Salt and black pepper	
1	Small egg, beaten with	1
	2 Tbsp milk	2 Tbsp
	Plaice (flounder),	
2	filleted	2
2 Tbsp	Butter, melted	2 Tbsp
1 Tbsp	Olive oil	1 Tbsp
	Small onion, sliced and	
1	pushed out into rings	1
	Small green pepper, pith removed, seeded	
1	and sliced	1
	Large tomatoes, blanched, peeled and	
2	sliced	2
	Black olives, stoned	
6	(pitted) and halved	6

Preheat oven to 230°C/450°F (gas mark 8).

On a large plate, combine breadcrumbs, parsley, garlic, lemon zest, salt and pepper. Place egg and milk mixture on another plate. Dip fish in egg then breadcrumbs, shaking off any excess. Arrange fish in a well-greased baking dish, in one layer. Sprinkle fish with the melted butter and bake for 15 minutes basting from time to time.

Meanwhile, heat the oil in a frying-pan and fry the onion and green pepper for 5

time to time. Remove from heat and keep hot.

Melt the remaining butter in a frying-pan and fry the mushrooms over moderate heat for 3 minutes, stirring. Stir in cream, wine, lemon juice, oregano and paprika and cook for a further 2 minutes. Do not boil.

Pour sauce over steaks and serve at once.

DALMATIAN FISH STEW

Metric/U.K.		U.S.
25g/1oz	Butter	2 Tbsp
1 Tbsp	Vegetable oil	1 Tbsp
1	Small onion, thinly sliced	1
¼kg/½lb	Tomatoes, blanched, peeled and chopped	½lb
4 Tbsp	White wine or water	4 Tbsp
2 tsp	White wine vinegar	2 tsp
¼ tsp	Chilli powder	¼ tsp
	Salt and black pepper	
¼ tsp	Dried tarragon	¼ tsp
1 Tbsp	Flour	1 Tbsp
2	Cod steaks	2

Melt half the butter and half the oil and fry the onion for 5 minutes. Add tomatoes, wine or water, vinegar, chilli powder, salt, pepper and tarragon. Bring to the boil, reduce heat to low, cover and simmer for 30 minutes.

Meanwhile, place flour on a plate and coat fish in flour, shaking off any excess. Melt the remaining butter and remaining oil in a frying-pan and fry the fish over moderate heat for 5 minutes on each side. Add more butter if necessary. Transfer fish to a serving dish, pour over sauce and serve at once.

CANNELLONI

A mock version of cannelloni, using pancake (crêpes) instead of pasta.

Metric/U.K.		U.S.
6	Pancakes (crêpes) made with Savoury pancake (crêpe) batter (see page 12) and kept hot	6
300ml/½ pint	Cheese sauce (see page 12)	1¼ cups
	Grated nutmeg	

minutes. Add tomatoes and olives. Reduce heat to low and simmer, uncovered, for 10 minutes, stirring from time to time.

Pour sauce over fish and serve at once.

SALMON STEAKS WITH MUSHROOM AND CREAM SAUCE

Metric/U.K.		U.S.
2	Salmon steaks	2
	Salt and black pepper	
50g/2oz	Butter	¼ cup
1 Tbsp	Chopped parsley	1 Tbsp
100g/¼lb	Mushrooms, wiped clean and sliced	1 cup
75ml/3floz	Double (heavy) cream	⅓ cup
2 Tbsp	Dry white wine	2 Tbsp
1 Tbsp	Lemon juice	1 Tbsp
¼ tsp	Dried oregano	¼ tsp
½ tsp	Paprika	½ tsp

Rub the salmon steaks all over with salt and pepper and arrange in a greased flameproof dish. Dot with half the butter and sprinkle over parsley. Cook under a hot grill (broiler) for 8 minutes on each side, basting from

1 Tbsp	Grated Parmesan cheese	1 Tbsp
FILLING		
	Small onion, finely	
1	chopped	1
1	Garlic clove, crushed	1
2 Tbsp	Vegetable oil	2 Tbsp
¼kg/½lb	Minced (ground) beef	½lb
¼ tsp	Dried thyme	¼ tsp
1 tsp	Dried basil	1 tsp
2 tsp	Tomato purée (paste)	2 tsp
	Canned peeled tomatoes	
200g/7oz	with their can juice	7oz
	Salt and black pepper	

For the filling, heat the oil in a frying-pan and fry the onion and garlic for 5 minutes. Add beef and fry for 5 minutes. Stir in thyme, basil, tomato purée (paste), tomatoes and their can juice, salt and pepper. Bring to the boil, reduce heat to low, cover and simmer for 30 minutes.

Preheat the oven to 220°C/425°F (gas mark 7). Lay pancakes (crêpes) out flat and spread a little of the filling on each. Roll up and arrange in a greased ovenproof dish. Pour over cheese sauce and sprinkle with nutmeg and cheese. Bake for 30 minutes until top is golden.

Serve at once.

SPAGHETTI WITH BACON AND TOMATO SAUCE

Metric/U.K.		U.S.
1 Tbsp	Olive oil	1 Tbsp
	Small onion, thinly	
1	sliced	1
1	Garlic clove, crushed	1
	Lean bacon slices, rinds	
3	removed and diced	3
2 Tbsp	Dry white wine	2 Tbsp
	Canned peeled	
200g/7oz	tomatoes, drained	7oz
	Salt and black pepper	
¼ tsp	Dried oregano	¼ tsp
175g/6oz	Spaghetti	6oz
50g/2oz	Grated Parmesan cheese	½ cup

Heat the oil in a saucepan and fry the onion and garlic over moderate heat for 5 minutes. Stir in bacon and cook for 4 minutes. Add wine, tomatoes, salt, pepper and oregano. Bring to the boil, reduce heat to low, cover and simmer for 15 minutes.

Meanwhile, cook the spaghetti. Fill a large saucepan two-thirds full of boiling

salted water. Bring to the boil and add spaghetti. Reduce heat to low, cover and simmer for 10 minutes. Drain and pile into a serving dish. Pour over sauce, sprinkle with cheese and serve at once.

SPAGHETTI WITH BUTTER AND CHEESE

Spaghetti is often served this way in Italy, for a first course. It makes a quick, tasty supper served with a mixed salad.

Metric/U.K.		U.S.
175g/6oz	Spaghetti	6oz
75g/3oz	Butter	⅓ cup
100g/¼lb	Grated Parmesan cheese	1 cup

Fill a large saucepan two-thirds full of boiling salted water. Bring to the boil and add spaghetti. Reduce heat to low, cover and simmer for 10 minutes.
Drain and pile into a serving dish. Add butter and half the cheese. Toss well until butter and cheese have melted. Serve at once, with remaining cheese in a separate bowl.

NOODLES WITH HAM

Metric/U.K.		U.S.
175g/6oz	Noodles	6oz
25g/1oz	Butter	2 Tbsp
	Salt and black pepper	
½ tsp	Dried basil	½ tsp
	Cooked lean ham, cut	
100g/¼lb	into thin strips	¼lb
	Garlic sausage, cut	
100g/¼lb	into thin strips	¼lb
	Large tomatoes,	
	blanched, peeled and	
2	cut into strips	2

Fill a large saucepan two-thirds full of boiling water. Bring to the boil, add noodles, reduce heat to low, cover and simmer for 10 minutes. Drain, return to rinsed out pan and add butter. Heat over very low heat until butter has melted. Toss noodles to coat in butter. Add salt, pepper, basil, ham, sausage and tomatoes. Increase heat to moderate and cook for 5 minutes, stirring frequently. Transfer to a serving dish and serve at once.

Left: *Cannelloni*

Lasagne

	Canned peeled tomatoes with their	
200g/7oz	can juice	7oz
2 Tbsp	Tomato purée (paste)	2 Tbsp
2 Tbsp	Single (light) cream	2 Tbsp

For the sauce, heat the oil and fry the onion, garlic, carrot and celery for 5 minutes over moderate heat. Add bacon and mushrooms and cook, stirring from time to time, for 5 minutes. Add beef and cook for 5 minutes. Stir in oregano, basil, salt, pepper, tomatoes with their can juice and tomato purée (paste). Bring to the boil, reduce heat to low, cover and simmer for 1 hour. Remove from heat and stir in cream. Set aside.

Half fill a large saucepan with boiling water and add half the olive oil. Bring to the boil, add half the lasagne, reduce heat to low, cover and simmer for 12 minutes. Carefully remove lasagne from water, being careful not to tear sheets, and lay flat to drain on a clean tea cloth. Add remaining oil to water and cook remaining lasagne in the same way.

Preheat the oven to 180°C/350°F (gas mark 4). Spoon half the meat sauce into a shallow ovenproof dish. Pour over half the béchamel sauce and sprinkle with one-third of the cheese. Cover with half the lasagne. Repeat these layers, finishing with a layer of cheese. Bake for 40 minutes. Serve at once.

LASAGNE

Metric/U.K.		U.S.
2 Tbsp	Olive oil	2 Tbsp
100g/¼lb	Lasagne	¼lb
300ml/½ pint	Béchamel sauce (see page 13)	1¼ cups
50g/2oz	Grated Parmesan cheese	½ cup
SAUCE		
2 Tbsp	Vegetable oil	2 Tbsp
1	Small onion, thinly sliced	1
1	Garlic clove, crushed	1
1	Small carrot, scraped and chopped	1
1	Celery stalk, chopped	1
2	Streaky (fatty) bacon slices, rinds removed and chopped	2
100g/¼lb	Mushrooms, wiped clean and sliced	1 cup
350g/¾lb	Minced (ground) beef	¾lb
a pinch	Dried oregano	a pinch
a pinch	Dried basil	a pinch
	Salt and black pepper	

LAMB PILAFF

Metric/U.K.		U.S.
25g/1oz	Butter	2 Tbsp
½kg/1lb	Boned leg of lamb, cut into 2·5cm/1 inch cubes	1lb
1	Garlic clove, crushed	1
1	Small green pepper, pith removed, seeded and thinly sliced	1
150ml/¼ pint	Red wine or chicken stock	⅔ cup
200g/7oz	Canned peeled tomatoes, drained	7oz
	Salt and black pepper	
⅛ tsp	Ground ginger	⅛ tsp
½ tsp	Ground saffron	½ tsp
175g/6oz	Long-grain rice	1 cup
150ml/¼ pint	Chicken stock	⅔ cup

Melt the butter in a flameproof casserole and fry the lamb for 5 minutes over moderate heat, turning to brown all over. Push lamb to one side and fry garlic and green pepper for 5 minutes. Pour in wine or stock and add tomatoes, salt, pepper, ginger, and saffron. Stir well and bring to the boil. Reduce heat to low, cover and simmer for 30 minutes.

Add rice and stock and bring back to the boil. Stir well, cover, reduce heat to low and simmer for 30 minutes. Serve at once.

PORK-FRIED RICE

Metric/U.K.		U.S.
1½ Tbsp	Vegetable oil	1½ Tbsp
1	Small onion, finely chopped	1
1	Celery stalk, finely chopped	1
1	Carrot, scraped and finely chopped	1
100g/¼lb	Cooked roast pork, cut into thin strips	¼lb
100g/¼lb	Small cabbage, finely shredded	¼lb
⅛ tsp	Black pepper	⅛ tsp
1 Tbsp	Soy sauce	1 Tbsp
100g/¼lb	Cooked long-grain rice	1½ cups
2	Eggs, lightly beaten	2
	Salt	

Heat 1 tablespoon of the oil in a large frying-pan and fry the onion, celery and carrot for 5 minutes over moderate heat, stirring constantly. Stir in pork, cabbage, pepper, soy sauce and rice and cook, stirring for 2 minutes. Moisten with a little water or chicken stock if the mixture is too dry. Set aside and keep hot.

Heat the remaining oil in a small frying-pan over moderate heat. Add eggs and salt and cook for 2 minutes. Turn the omelette over and cook the other side for 2 minutes. Remove from pan and cut into small strips.

Spoon rice mixture into a serving dish and garnish with omelette strips. Serve at once.

VEGETABLE CURRY

Metric/U.K.		U.S.
2 Tbsp	Vegetable oil	2 Tbsp
1	Medium-sized onion, finely chopped	1

Vegetable Curry

Metric/U.K.		U.S.
1cm/½in piece	Fresh root ginger peeled and finely chopped	½in piece
1	Garlic clove, finely crushed	1
1	Fresh green chilli, finely chopped	1
½ tsp	Turmeric	½ tsp
2 tsp	Ground coriander	2 tsp
2 tsp	Paprika	2 tsp
¼ tsp	Cayenne pepper	¼ tsp
a pinch	Ground fenugreek	a pinch
	Black pepper	
1 Tbsp	Lemon juice	1 Tbsp
¼kg/½lb	Potatoes, peeled and cubed	½lb
100g/¼lb	Turnips, peeled and cubed	¼lb
100g/¼lb	Carrots, scraped and sliced	¼lb
50g/2oz	French (green) beans, sliced	2oz
50g/2oz	Frozen peas, thawed	2oz
	Salt	

200g/7oz	Canned peeled tomatoes, rubbed through strainer with their can juice	7oz

Heat the oil in a large saucepan and fry onion, ginger, garlic and chilli over moderate heat for 8 minutes.

Meanwhile, in a small bowl, combine turmeric, coriander, paprika, cayenne, fenugreek and pepper. Stir in lemon juice and water, if necessary, to make a smooth paste. Add paste to pan and fry for 5 minutes, stirring constantly. Add potatoes, turnips, carrots, beans and peas and fry for 5 minutes, stirring. Stir in salt and strained tomatoes. Bring to the boil, reduce heat to low, cover and simmer for 30 minutes.

Transfer curry to a serving dish and serve at once.

MADRAS CHICKEN CURRY

A really fiery curry for experienced eaters. Creamed coconut can be bought from Indian food stores.

Metric/U.K.		U.S.
2 Tbsp	Vegetable oil	2 Tbsp
½ tsp	Mustard seeds	½ tsp
1	Medium-sized onion, finely chopped	1
1cm/½in piece	Fresh root ginger, peeled and finely chopped	½in piece
2	Garlic cloves, crushed	2
1 tsp	Turmeric	1 tsp
2 tsp	Ground coriander	2 tsp
½ tsp	Hot chilli powder	½ tsp
a pinch	Ground fenugreek	a pinch
1 tsp	Ground cumin	1 tsp
	Black pepper	
4	Small chicken pieces, skinned	4
300ml/½ pint	Coconut milk, made	1¼ cups
40g/1½oz	from creamed coconut	3 Tbsp
300ml/½ pint	dissolved in hot water	1¼ cups
	Salt	
1	Bay leaf	1
1	Fresh green chilli, slit and seeds removed	1
2 Tbsp	Lemon juice	2 Tbsp

Heat the oil in a large saucepan and add mustard seeds. Heat over moderate heat until seeds begin to pop. Reduce heat to low and fry onion, ginger and garlic for 8 minutes. Add turmeric, coriander, chilli powder, fenugreek, cumin and black pepper. Fry spices for 5 minutes. If mixture begins to stick to the pan, add a little water.

Add chicken and fry for 5 minutes, turning to brown on all sides. Pour in coconut milk, and add salt, bay leaf and chilli. Stir, bring to the boil, reduce heat to low, cover and simmer for 1 hour. Uncover the pan 15 minutes before the end of the cooking time. Stir in lemon juice.

Remove bay leaf and serve.

POTATO OMELETTE

Metric/U.K.		U.S.
40g/1½oz	Butter	3 Tbsp
2	Medium-sized potatoes, peeled and chopped	2
6	Eggs	6
	Salt and black pepper	
2 Tbsp	Cold water	2 Tbsp
1 Tbsp	Chopped parsley	1 Tbsp

Melt 25 g/1 oz (2 Tbsp) of the butter in a small frying-pan and fry the potatoes for 10 minutes, turning to cook evenly. Remove pan from heat and keep potatoes hot.

In a bowl, beat eggs, salt, pepper, water and parsley together. Melt the remaining butter in an omelette pan over moderate heat. Pour in egg mixture and leave for a few seconds. Reduce heat to low, lift edges of the omelette and tilt pan so that liquid egg runs on to the pan. Put pan down flat and leave until omelette begins to set again. Spoon over potatoes, then flip one half of the omelette over the other. Slide on to a serving plate, cut in 2 and serve at once.

HADDOCK AND CHEESE OMELETTE

Metric/U.K.		U.S.
40g/1½oz	Butter	3 Tbsp
100g/¼lb	Smoked haddock, cooked and flaked	¼lb
150ml/¼ pint	Double (heavy) cream	⅔ cup
6	Eggs, separated	6
3 Tbsp	Grated Parmesan cheese	3 Tbsp
	Salt and black pepper	
1 Tbsp	Chopped parsley	1 Tbsp

Melt 25g/1 oz (2 Tbsp) of the butter in a small frying-pan and fry the haddock and 2 tablespoons cream for 1 minute.

In a large bowl, beat egg yolks with half the cheese, salt, pepper and parsley. Add fish mixture.

In another large bowl beat the egg whites until stiff, then fold whites into fish mixture.

Melt the remaining butter in an omelette pan over moderate heat. Pour in egg mixture and leave for 2 minutes. Sprinkle with remaining cheese and pour over remaining cream. Cook the omelette under a hot grill (broiler) for 30 seconds. Transfer to a serving plate, cut in 2 and serve at once.

VEGETABLE PAELLA

Metric/U.K.		U.S.
4 Tbsp	Olive oil	4 Tbsp
1	Large onion, thinly sliced	1
1	Garlic clove, crushed	1
1	Small red pepper, pith removed, seeded and sliced	1
175g/6oz	Long-grain rice	1 cup
300ml/½ pint	Vegetable or chicken stock	1¼ cups

Potato Omelette

Metric/U.K.		U.S.
2	Large tomatoes, blanched, peeled and chopped	2
50g/2oz	Frozen green beans, thawed	2oz
25g/1oz	Frozen peas, thawed	2 Tbsp
1	Celery stalk, chopped	1
8	Black olives, stoned (pitted) and halved	8
	Salt and black pepper	
$\frac{1}{8}$ tsp	Crushed saffron threads, soaked	$\frac{1}{8}$ tsp
1 tsp	in hot water	1 tsp
2 Tbsp	Slivered almonds	2 Tbsp

Heat the oil in a large saucepan and fry onion, garlic and red pepper for 5 minutes over moderate heat. Stir in rice and cook for 5 minutes, stirring from time to time. Pour in stock and stir in tomatoes, beans, peas, celery, olives, salt and pepper. Drain the saffron and stir infused liquid into pan. Discard saffron threads. Bring to the boil, reduce heat to low, cover and simmer for 30 minutes.

Turn paella into a serving dish, sprinkle over almonds and serve at once.

PIZZA WITH ANCHOVIES AND TUNA

Mozzarella is the ideal cheese for pizza toppings as it melts so beautifully.

Metric/U.K.		U.S.
	Pizza dough (see Peperoni pizza below)	
FILLING		
2 Tbsp	Olive oil	2 Tbsp
2	Small onions, sliced and pushed out into rings	2
400g/14oz	Canned peeled tomatoes with their can juice	14oz
1 Tbsp	Tomato purée (paste)	1 Tbsp
	Black pepper	
1 Tbsp	Chopped parsley	1 Tbsp
100g/$\frac{1}{4}$lb	Canned tuna, drained and flaked	$\frac{1}{4}$lb
175g/6oz	Mozzarella cheese, thinly sliced	6oz
6	Canned anchovy fillets, drained and halved	6
4	Green stuffed olives, halved	4

First make the dough as described under Peperoni Pizza below.

Heat half the oil in a saucepan and fry the onions over moderate heat for 5 minutes. Stir in tomatoes, their can juice, tomato purée (paste) and pepper. Bring to the boil, reduce heat to low, cover and simmer for 30 minutes. Stir in parsley and tuna and remove pan from heat.

Preheat oven to 230°C/450°F (gas mark 8). Grease a baking sheet with a little of the remaining oil. Turn dough out on to a floured surface and knead for 3 minutes. Divide in half and roll out each half to a circle, 6 mm/$\frac{1}{4}$ inch thick. Arrange circles on the baking sheet and spoon over tomato sauce. Top with cheese slices and arrange anchovy fillets and olives on top. Sprinkle with remaining oil and bake for 20 minutes. Serve at once.

PEPERONI PIZZA

Metric/U.K.		U.S.
15g/$\frac{1}{2}$oz	Fresh yeast	1 Tbsp
$\frac{1}{4}$ tsp	Sugar	$\frac{1}{4}$ tsp

and smooth. Rinse, dry and lightly grease mixing bowl, shape dough into a ball and return to bowl. Dust with flour and cover with a damp tea cloth. Put in a warm place for 1 hour.

Meanwhile make the filling. Heat 2 Tbsp of the oil in a saucepan and fry the onion and garlic over moderate heat for 5 minutes. Add tomatoes, their can juice, salt, pepper, tomato purée (paste), half the basil and oregano, and bay leaf. Stir well. Bring to the boil, reduce heat to low, cover pan and simmer for 30 minutes. Remove and discard bay leaf.

Preheat oven to 230°C/450°F (gas mark 8). Grease a baking sheet with a little of the remaining oil. Turn dough out on to a floured surface and knead for 3 minutes. Divide in half and roll out each half to a circle, 6 mm/¼ inch thick. Arrange circles on the baking sheet and spoon over tomato sauce. Top with cheese slices. Sprinkle with parsley, the remaining basil and oregano and top with sausage slices. Sprinkle with remaining oil then bake for 20 minutes. Serve at once.

Left: *Peperoni Pizza*

QUICHE LORRAINE

A classic favourite. Make sure the cheese is thinly sliced or it could make the pastry underneath a little soggy. It is equally delicious hot or cold.

9 Tbsp	Lukewarm water	9 Tbsp
¼kg/½lb	Flour	2 cups
	Salt	
FILLING		
3 Tbsp	Olive oil	3 Tbsp
1	Small onion, sliced	1
1	Garlic clove, crushed	1
	Canned peeled	
	tomatoes with their	
400g/14oz	can juice	14oz
	Salt and black pepper	
1 Tbsp	Tomato purée (paste)	1 Tbsp
½ tsp	Dried basil	½ tsp
½ tsp	Dried oregano	½ tsp
1	Bay leaf	1
	Mozzarella cheese,	
175g/6oz	sliced	6oz
1 Tbsp	Chopped parsley	1 Tbsp
1	Peperoni sausage, sliced	1

Cream yeast, sugar and 1 Tbsp water together. Put in a warm place for 15 minutes until frothy.

Sift flour and salt into a warmed mixing bowl. Make a well in the centre and pour in yeast mixture and remaining water. Mix to a dough, then knead on a floured surface for 10 minutes. The dough should be elastic

Metric/U.K.		U.S.
	Shortcrust pastry (see	
100g/¼lb	page 13)	¼lb
	Gruyère or Cheddar	
50g/2oz	cheese, thinly sliced	2oz
	Lean bacon slices,	
	grilled (broiled) until	
4	crisp and crumbled	4
75ml/3floz	Single (light) cream	⅓ cup
2	Eggs	2
	Salt and white pepper	

Line a 15 cm/6 inch flan dish with the pastry, then chill in the refrigerator for 30 minutes.

Preheat the oven to 200°C/400°F (gas mark 6). Cover the bottom of the flan case with cheese then bacon. Beat the cream, eggs, salt and pepper together and pour into case. Place dish on a baking sheet and bake for 25 minutes or until filling is set. Serve at once.

DESSERTS

DATES STUFFED WITH MARZIPAN

This recipe makes 24 stuffed dates, but they will keep, wrapped in foil and put in an airtight container for several days.

Metric/U.K.		U.S.
24	Dates	24
	MARZIPAN	
50g/2oz	Ground almonds	½ cup
50g/2oz	Caster (superfine) sugar	¼ cup
½	Egg white, lightly beaten	½
1 tsp	Rum or sherry	1 tsp
1 tsp	Almond extract	1 tsp
2 to 3 drops	Red or green food colouring (optional)	2 to 3 drops
6	Walnuts, quartered	6

For the marzipan, mix together ground almonds and sugar. Beat in egg white, rum or sherry and almond extract. Add colouring if using it, and knead well.

Slit the dates lengthways across the top

and remove stones (pits). Divide marzipan into 24 equal pieces and shape each piece into an oval. Insert marzipan into dates and press a walnut quarter on top of marzipan. Put stuffed dates into paper cases and arrange on a serving plate.

DATE AND BANANA DESSERT

Metric/U.K.		U.S.
3	Bananas, sliced	3
	Dates, stoned (pitted)	
¼kg/½lb	and halved	½lb
	Satsumas or tangerines, peeled, pith removed	
2	and segmented	2
150ml/¼ pint	Single (light) cream	⅔ cup
	Plain (semi-sweet)	
15g/½oz	chocolate, grated	½ square

Arrange half the banana slices in the bottom of a serving dish and pour over a quarter of the cream. Cover with half the dates and more cream. Arrange half the satsumas or tangerines over the cream and top with more cream. Finish making layers, ending with cream. Chill in the refrigerator for 1 hour.

Sprinkle with grated chocolate and serve at once.

BAKED APPLES

These old friends can be filled with numerous flavourings, such as treacle (molasses), golden (maple) syrup, nuts, fruit peel, honey and fresh fruits. Serve hot or cold.

Metric/U.K.		U.S.
	Large tart dessert	
2	apples, cored	2
	Soft (light) brown	
2 Tbsp	sugar	2 Tbsp
2 tsp	Mixed dried fruit	2 tsp
15g/½oz	Butter	1 Tbsp

Preheat the oven to 180°C/350°F (gas mark 4).

Peel off about 2.5 cm/1 inch of skin from the tops of the apples. Arrange apples in a baking dish and fill centres with sugar and fruit. Dot with butter.

Pour enough hot water into the dish to

come 1 cm /½ inch up the sides of the apples. Bake for 30 minutes, basting frequently. Serve at once.

Baked Apples

APPLE MOUSSE

Metric/U.K.		U.S.
	Tart dessert apples,	
½kg/1lb	quartered	1lb
225ml/6floz	Cider (sweet or dry)	¾ cup
	Sugar	
¼ tsp	Vanilla extract	¼ tsp
150ml/¼ pint	Double (heavy) cream	⅔ cup

Put apples in a saucepan, pour in cider and bring to the boil. Reduce heat to low, cover and simmer for 25 minutes or until soft. Rub apple and cider mixture through a

October Cobbler

strainer. Discard contents of strainer. Measure pulp and to every 100 g/¼ lb add 25 g/1 oz (2 tsp) sugar.

Return apple pulp to pan and cook over low heat, stirring to dissolve sugar. Bring to the boil and boil rapidly for 10 minutes or until very thick.

Spoon mixture into a bowl and allow to cool. Place the bowl in another larger bowl with ice cubes in it and whisk the apple mixture. Beat half the cream until thick and fold into the apple mixture with the vanilla extract. Spoon into individual dishes, top with remaining cream and serve at once.

OCTOBER COBBLER

Metric/U.K.		U.S.
¼kg/½lb	Blackberries,	½lb
	Large tart dessert	
	apple, peeled, cored	
1	and chopped	1
1½ Tbsp	Water	1½ Tbsp
2 Tbsp	Soft (light) brown sugar	2 Tbsp
1 tsp	Grated orange zest	1 tsp
a pinch	Ground cinnamon	a pinch
1 tsp	Arrowroot dissolved in ½ Tbsp fresh orange juice	1 tsp
100g/¼lb	Shortcrust pastry (see page 13)	¼lb
1	Small egg yolk beaten with 1 Tbsp milk	1
1 Tbsp	sugar	1 Tbsp

Preheat the oven to 200°C/400°F (gas mark 6).

Place blackberries, apple, water, sugar, orange zest and cinnamon in a saucepan and bring to the boil over moderate heat, stirring. Reduce heat to low, cover and simmer for 5 minutes. Stir in dissolved arrowroot and cook, stirring constantly, for 2 minutes. Spoon mixture into a small pie dish.

Roll out the dough on a floured surface to 6 mm/¼ inch thick. Using a 5 cm/2 inch cutter, cut dough into circles. Re-roll trimmings and roll out to 3 mm/⅛ inch thick. Trim to a strip 1.25 cm/½ inch wide. Dampen rim of pie dish and press strip on to rim. Dampen strip and press circles, overlapping slightly, on to strip, leaving a gap in the middle. Prick circles with a fork and brush with egg and milk mixture.

Sprinkle with sugar and bake for 25 minutes. Serve at once.

MINCEMEAT AND APPLE CRUMBLE

The weight of the apples is calculated after peeling and coring.

Metric/U.K.		U.S.
	Tart dessert apples, peeled, cored and	
¼kg/½lb	sliced	½lb
1 Tbsp	Sugar	1 Tbsp
100g/¼lb	Mincemeat	½ cup
1 tsp	Grated lemon zest	1 tsp
¼ tsp	Mixed spice	¼ tsp

Mincemeat and Apple Crumble

1 Tbsp	Water	1 Tbsp
CRUMBLE		
100g/¼lb	Flour	1 cup
¼ tsp	Mixed spice	¼ tsp
50g/2oz	Butter	¼ cup
50g/2oz	Sugar	¼ cup
1 tsp	Grated lemon zest	1 tsp

Put apples and sugar in a saucepan, cover with water and bring to the boil. Reduce heat to moderate, partially cover and simmer for 10 minutes. Drain apples and discard cooking liquid.

Preheat the oven to 180°C/350°F (gas mark 4). For the crumble, sift flour and mixed spice into a bowl and rub in butter until mixture resembles fine breadcrumbs. Stir in sugar and lemon zest.

Combine apples, mincemeat, lemon zest, mixed spice and water and spoon into a greased baking dish.

Cover apple mixture with crumble. Bake for 45 minutes. Serve at once.

INSTANT YOGHURT PUDDING

Metric/U.K.		U.S.
2	Small bananas, thinly sliced	2
1	Large orange, peeled, pith removed and segmented	1
300ml/½ pint	Plain yoghurt	1¼ cups
2 Tbsp	Soft (light) brown sugar	2 Tbsp

Place the bananas and orange in a flame-proof dish. Pour over the yoghurt and toss well to mix. Sprinkle with sugar.

Heat under a hot grill (broiler) for 3 to 4 minutes or until sugar caramelizes. Serve at once.

JAM OMELETTE

Metric/U.K.		U.S.
4	Eggs	4
2 Tbsp	Caster (superfine) sugar	2 Tbsp
a pinch	Salt	a pinch
25g/1oz	Butter	2 Tbsp
2 Tbsp	Raspberry jam	2 Tbsp

In a mixing bowl beat the egg, a little of the sugar and salt together with a wire whisk.

Melt the butter in a small frying-pan over moderate heat. Pour in egg mixture and leave for a few seconds. Reduce heat to low, lift edges of the omelette and tilt the pan so that liquid egg runs on to the pan. Put pan down flat and leave until omelette begins to set again. Place jam on one half of the omelette, then flip over the other half. Slide on to a flameproof serving plate.

Sprinkle with remaining sugar and place under a hot grill (broiler) for 1 minute. Cut in 2 and serve at once.

PANCAKE (CRÊPES) WITH MAPLE SYRUP

Try making traditional American pancakes (crêpes) by using buttermilk instead of milk, 1 egg and twice as much butter.

Metric/U.K.		U.S.
100ml/4floz	Pancakes (crêpes) made with Sweet pancake (crêpe) batter (see page 12)	½ cup
SAUCE		
50ml/2floz	Maple syrup	¼ cup
1 tsp	Grated lemon zest	1 tsp
1 Tbsp	Lemon juice	1 Tbsp

Fry the pancakes (crêpes) and keep hot.

To make the sauce, heat the syrup in a saucepan over low heat, stirring frequently, until thin. Remove pan from heat and stir in lemon zest and juice. Serve at once, with the pancakes (crêpes).

ICE-CREAM CRÊPES

Metric/U.K.		U.S.
8	Pancakes (crêpes) made from sweet pancake (crêpe) batter (see page 12)	8
150ml/¼ pint	Vanilla ice-cream (see page 13)	⅔ cup
200g/7oz	Canned or fresh peach slices, drained	7oz

Fry the pancakes (crêpes) and allow to cool.

Lay pancakes (crêpes) out flat and spoon a little ice-cream and a few peach slices on to each pancake (crêpe). Roll up and serve.

ORANGE CARAMEL TRIFLE

True trifles are based on sponge, alcohol, fresh custard made with eggs, fresh fruit and cream. This trifle has other even grander additions, making it a very special dessert.

Metric/U.K.		U.S.			
3	Trifle sponge squares, sliced in half Orange-flavoured	3			
		2 Tbsp	liqueur or sherry	2 Tbsp	
		1 Tbsp	Fresh orange juice	1 Tbsp	
		100g/¼lb	Sugar	½ cup	
			Custard (see Lemon bread pudding page 148) using half quantities		
		2	Oranges, peeled, pith removed and thinly sliced	2	
		150ml/¼ pint	Double (heavy) cream, stiffly whipped	⅔ cup	

Orange Caramel Trifle

Strawberries and Cream Chantilly

Metric/U.K.		U.S.
1 Tbsp	Caster (superfine) sugar	1 Tbsp
2 or 3 drops	Vanilla extract	2 or 3 drops

Arrange the strawberries in 2 individual serving dishes and set aside.

Pour cream into a cooled mixing bowl. Whip slowly until just slightly thickened. Fold in sugar and vanilla extract.

Pour over strawberries and serve at once.

BANANA FLUFF

Metric/U.K.		U.S.
25g/1oz	Caster (superfine) sugar	2 Tbsp
2	Eggs, separated	2
10g/⅓oz	Butter	¼ Tbsp
1	Large banana, sliced	1
1 Tbsp	Brandy	1 Tbsp
½ tsp	Icing (confectioners') sugar	½ tsp

Whisk the sugar and egg yolks together until smooth. Stiffly beat the egg whites and fold into yolk mixture. Melt the butter in a 25 cm (10 in) frying-pan over low heat, turning pan to coat all over in butter. Pour in egg mixture and leave to cook for 6 minutes, without stirring.

Rub the banana through a strainer into a bowl. Discard contents of strainer. Stir in brandy.

Spoon banana purée into centre of egg. Flip one half over the other and slide on to a serving plate. Sprinkle with sugar, cut in 2 and serve at once.

VANILLA SOUFFLÉ

Metric/U.K.		U.S.
1 Tbsp	Icing (confectioners') sugar	1 Tbsp
150ml/¼ pint	Milk	⅔ cup
1	Vanilla pod	1
15g/½oz	Butter	1 Tbsp
2 Tbsp	Flour	2 Tbsp
1	Egg yolk	1
2 tsp	Sugar	2 tsp
3	Egg whites	3

Place a large baking sheet in the oven and preheat oven to 180°C/350°F (gas mark 4). Grease a 900 ml/1½ pint (1 quart) soufflé dish. Sprinkle with icing (confectioners')

Place sponge in the bottom of a trifle or dish. Sprinkle over liqueur or sherry and orange juice and set aside for 30 minutes.

In a heavy saucepan heat the sugar over low heat, shaking the pan from time to time, until it has melted. Increase heat to moderate and boil the syrup, shaking pan from time to time, until it turns a rich golden brown. Place pan in a bowl of hot water to keep caramel hot.

Cover sponge with a little custard then cover with some of the orange slices. Trickle over a little of the caramel. Make alternate layers, finishing with caramel-coated orange slices. Chill in the refrigerator for 2 hours.

Pipe cream using a forcing bag and star nozzle over trifle in decorative swirls. Serve at once.

STRAWBERRIES AND CREAM CHANTILLY

Metric/U.K.		U.S.
¼kg/½lb	Strawberries, hulled	½lb
150ml/¼ pint	Double (heavy) cream	⅔ cup

sugar, knocking out any excess.

Scald milk and vanilla pod, cover and set aside to infuse for 20 minutes. Remove vanilla pod.

Melt the butter over moderate heat and stir in flour. Cook for 1 minute. Off the heat, gradually stir in milk. Cook for 2 minutes, stirring constantly. Allow sauce to cool. Beat egg yolk with sugar and stir into sauce. Beat egg whites until stiff. Using a large metal spoon, carefully fold the whites into the sauce. Quickly spoon into prepared dish. Carefully slide dish on to baking sheet. Bake in centre of oven for 25 minutes, or until soufflé has risen and is golden on top. Serve at once.

MIDSUMMER FLAN

Metric/U.K.		U.S.
	Digestive biscuits (graham crackers),	
75g/3oz	crushed	¾ cup
½ tsp	Grated orange zest	½ tsp
40g/1½oz	Butter	3 Tbsp
1 Tbsp	Caster (superfine) sugar	1 Tbsp
	Mixed apricot halves,	
¼kg/½lb	raspberries and grapes	½lb
1½ Tbsp	Redcurrant jelly	1½ Tbsp
1 Tbsp	Water	1 Tbsp

Preheat the oven to 180°C/350°F (gas mark 4).

Mix together biscuits (crackers) and orange zest. Melt the butter and add the sugar. Pour over biscuits (crackers) and mix thoroughly. Line a small flan dish with the crumb mixture. Bake for 10 minutes, cool and allow to become cold.

Arrange fruits decoratively over the crumb case. Warm redcurrant jelly and water together, cool to lukewarm then brush over the fruit. Leave to set for 30 minutes before serving.

GRILLED (BROILED) FRUIT SALAD PACKETS

This is an excellent way of preserving goodness and flavour during cooking. Use any good combination of fresh or canned fruit.

Midsummer Flan

Metric/U.K.		U.S.
	Small sweet dessert apple, peeled, cored	
1	and chopped	1
	Small orange, peeled, pith removed and	
1	segmented	1
	Canned pineapple	
2	slices, chopped	2
8	Seedless grapes halved	8
1 Tbsp	Seedless raisins	1 Tbsp
	Caster (superfine)	
1 Tbsp	sugar	1 Tbsp
2 or 3 drops	Vanilla extract	2 or 3 drops

Mix all the ingredients together in a bowl. Cut out 2 x 20 cm/8 inch squares of foil. Press a square of foil into your hand to form a cup shape. Spoon half the mixture into the foil, bring the edges up and crimp to seal. Make the other packet in the same way.

Place packets on a rack in a grill (broiler) pan. Cook under a hot grill (broiler) for 15 minutes or until very hot .Serve at once.

PINEAPPLE SOUFFLÉ

Below: Melon Surprise
Opposite Page:
Pineapple Souffle

Metric/U.K.		U.S.
25g/1oz	Butter	2 Tbsp
25g/1oz	Flour	¼ cup
¼ tsp	Ground allspice	¼ tsp
100ml/4floz	Single (light) cream	½ cup
2 Tbsp	Kirsch	2 Tbsp
2 Tbsp	Caster (superfine) sugar	2 Tbsp
	Fresh pineapple (peeled and cored weight),	
¼kg/½lb	finely chopped	½lb
2	Egg yolks	2
3	Egg whites	3

Place a large baking sheet in the oven and preheat the oven to 190°C/375°F (gas mark 5). Grease a 900 ml/1½ pint (1 quart) soufflé dish and attach a paper collar to protrude 5 cm/2 inches above the rim.

Melt the butter in a saucepan over moderate heat and stir in flour and allspice. Cook for 1 minute. Off the heat gradually stir in cream, then stir in kirsch, sugar and pineapple. Cook over low heat for 5 minutes, stirring constantly. Allow to cool then beat in egg yolks.

Beat the egg whites until stiff. Using a large metal spoon, carefully fold the whites into the sauce. Quickly spoon into prepared dish. Carefully slide dish onto baking sheet. Bake in the centre of the oven for 40 minutes, or until soufflé has risen and is golden brown on top. Serve at once.

MELON SURPRISE

Metric/U.K.		U.S.
1	Small melon	1

138

MELON BALLS IN WHITE WINE

Metric/U.K.		U.S.
	Small honeydew melon,	
1	halved and seeded	1
100ml/4floz	Sweet white wine	½ cup
	Mint leaves	

Use a melon baller to scoop out melon flesh into balls. Reserve shells. Place balls in a shallow dish and pour over wine. Chill in the refrigerator for 1 hour.

Spoon melon balls back into shells and spoon the liquid from the bowl over melon balls. Garnish with mint leaves and serve at once.

KNICKERBOCKER GLORY

Metric/U.K.		U.S.
	Strawberries, hulled	
100g/¼lb	and sliced	¼lb
	Vanilla ice-cream (see	
150ml/¼ pint	page 13)	⅔ cup
	Peaches, peeled, stoned	
2	(pitted) and sliced	2
150ml/¼ pint	Chocolate ice-cream	⅔ cup
2 Tbsp	Chocolate sauce	2 Tbsp
	Double (heavy) cream	
2 Tbsp	stiffly whipped	2 Tbsp
2	Glacé (candied) cherries	2

Place strawberries in the bottom of 2 tall sundae glasses. Top with a scoop of vanilla ice-cream then a layer of peaches. Cover with chocolate ice-cream and spoon over chocolate sauce.

Spoon or pipe over cream and top each with a cherry. Serve at once.

NUT AND APPLE CREAM

For a less rich dessert, use plain yoghurt instead of the cream.

Metric/U.K.		U.S.
	Tart dessert apples,	
	peeled, cored and	
½kg/1lb	sliced	1lb
½ tsp	Ground cinnamon	½ tsp
1	Clove	1
1 Tbsp	Sugar	1 Tbsp

Knickerbocker Glory

	Chopped preserved	
1 Tbsp	ginger	1 Tbsp
150ml/¼ pint	Ginger syrup from jar	⅔ cup
	Vanilla ice-cream	
150ml/¼ pint	(see page 13)	⅔ cup
	Crushed ice	

Cut a plug 5 cm/2 inches in diameter from the top of the melon, so that you can see through to the seed section. Set plug aside.

Remove seeds and filaments from the centre of the melon, being careful not to remove any flesh. Spoon ginger and syrup into melon and replace plug. Chill in the refrigerator for 1 hour.

Remove plug and spoon in ice-cream. To serve, cut melon open so that each half contains a portion of ginger and ice-cream. Serve on a bed of crushed ice.

1 tsp	Grated lemon zest	1 tsp
1 Tbsp	Lemon juice	1 Tbsp
2 Tbsp	Mixed nuts, chopped	2 Tbsp
75ml/3floz	Double (heavy) cream	⅓ cup
½ tsp	Grated nutmeg	½ tsp

Combine apples, cinnamon, clove and sugar in a saucepan and cook over moderate heat stirring frequently, for 10 minutes. Remove and discard clove. Rub apples through a strainer into a bowl. Discard contents of strainer.

Allow apple purée to cool. Stir in lemon rind, lemon juice and nuts, then fold in cream. Spoon into individual serving dishes and sprinkle with nutmeg. Chill for 1 hour in the refrigerator before serving.

GOOSEBERRY CREAM

Metric/U.K.		U.S.
¼kg/½lb	Gooseberries, trimmed	½lb
150ml/¼ pint	Water	⅔ cup
4 Tbsp	Dry white wine	4 Tbsp
1 tsp	Grated lemon zest	1 tsp
50g/2oz	Sugar	¼ cup
2	Small eggs, separated	2

Bring the gooseberries, water, wine and lemon zest to the boil in a saucepan over moderate heat. Reduce heat to low, cover and simmer for 20 minutes. Rub gooseberries through a strainer into a bowl. Discard contents of strainer.

Return purée to rinsed out pan and add sugar. Stir over low heat until sugar has dissolved. Allow to cool, then beat in egg yolks. Beat egg whites until stiff then fold into gooseberry mixture.

Spoon into individual serving dishes and chill in the refrigerator for 1 hour before serving.

AVOCADO CREAM

Always use fresh limes for the lime juice, if using; lime cordial or any other bottled or canned juice will not be effective.

Metric/U.K.		U.S.
	Large avocado, halved, peeled and stoned	
1	(pitted)	1
2 Tbsp	Caster (superfine) sugar	2 Tbsp
2 Tbsp	Lemon or lime juice	2 Tbsp
	Double (heavy) cream	
150ml/¼ pint	stiffly whipped	⅔ cup

Gooseberry Cream

Rub the avocado flesh through a strainer into a bowl. Discard contents of strainer. Stir in the sugar and lemon or lime juice.

Fold in the cream. Spoon avocado mixture into serving dishes and chill in the refrigerator for 1 hour before serving.

QUICK PEACH DESSERT

Metric/U.K.		U.S.
	Fresh peaches, peeled, halved and stoned	
2	(pitted)	2

Metric/U.K.		U.S.
1½ Tbsp	Double (heavy) cream	1½ Tbsp
2 tsp	Caster (superfine) sugar	2 tsp
a pinch	Vanilla extract	a pinch
15g/½oz	Plain (semi-sweet) chocolate, finely grated	½ square
2 Tbsp	Slivered almonds	2 Tbsp

Arrange peach halves, rounded sides down, in 2 individual serving dishes.

Whisk the cream and vanilla extract together until stiff. Fold in half the chocolate and half the almonds. Spoon a little of the cream on to each peach. Sprinkle with remaining chocolate and almonds and chill in the refrigerator for 1 hour before serving.

PEACH PIE

Metric/U.K.		U.S.
6	Peaches, peeled, stoned (pitted) and sliced	6
2 tsp	Flour	2 tsp
2 Tbsp	Soft (light) brown sugar	2 Tbsp
1 Tbsp	Butter, melted	1 Tbsp
¼ tsp	Vanilla extract	¼ tsp
1	Small egg beaten with 1 tsp milk	1
1 Tbsp	Slivered almonds	1 Tbsp
PASTRY		
25g/1oz	Butter, softened	2 Tbsp
50g/2oz	Cream cheese	¼ cup
50g/2oz	Flour	½ cup
1 Tbsp	Sugar	1 Tbsp
small pinch	Salt	small pinch
2 Tbsp	Double (heavy) cream	2 Tbsp

For the pastry, cream the butter and cheese together in a bowl. Sift flour, sugar and salt together and fold into cheese mixture. Fold in cream. Form into a dough and shape into a ball. Dust with flour and chill in the refrigerator for 30 minutes.

Preheat the oven to 180°C/350°F (gas mark 4). Combine peaches, flour, sugar, melted butter and vanilla extract and turn into a small pie dish.

Roll out the pastry on a floured surface, to 2.5 cm/1 inch larger than the top of the pie dish. Cut a 1.25 cm/½ inch strip around the pastry, dampen rim of the dish with water and press the pastry strip on the rim. Dampen the strip and lift dough onto the dish. Trim and crimp the edges to seal.

Quick Peach Dessert

Brush pastry with beaten egg and milk and sprinkle with the almonds. Cut 2 slits in the middle of the pastry. Bake for 45 minutes. Serve at once.

HONEY-BAKED PEARS

Metric/U.K.		U.S.
	Large firm pears, peeled,	
2	halved and cored	2
2 Tbsp	Lemon juice	2 Tbsp
2 Tbsp	Brandy, sherry or port	2 Tbsp
4 Tbsp	Clear honey	4 Tbsp
$\frac{1}{4}$ tsp	Ground cinnamon	$\frac{1}{4}$ tsp
a pinch	Grated nutmeg	a pinch
15g/$\frac{1}{2}$oz	Butter	1 Tbsp

Preheat the oven to 180°C/350°F (gas mark 4). Arrange the pear halves, cut sides down, in a greased baking dish.

Warm the lemon juice, brandy, sherry or port and honey together in a saucepan, stirring. Stir in cinnamon and nutmeg and remove from heat. Pour over pears, dot with butter and bake for 30 minutes. Serve at once.

PEARS BAKED WITH CARDAMOM

Metric/U.K.		U.S.
	Large pears, peeled,	
2	halved cored and sliced	2

Pears Baked with Cardamom

143

	Soft (light) brown	
1½ Tbsp	sugar	1½ Tbsp
	Fresh orange juice or	
	orange-flavoured	
6 Tbsp	liqueur	6 Tbsp
1½ tsp	Ground cardamom	1½ tsp
	Double (heavy) cream,	
150ml/¼ pint	stiffly whipped	⅔ cup

Preheat the oven to 180°C/350°F (gas mark 4). Arrange the pears in a shallow baking dish and sprinkle over the sugar. Pour orange juice or liqueur over the pears and sprinkle with cardamom.

Bake for 35 to 40 minutes or until pears are tender. Transfer to individual serving dishes, allow to cool, then chill in the refrigerator for 15 minutes. Top with cream and serve at once.

PEACH MELBA

If you are feeling extravagent, stir a little kirsch into the melba sauce before serving.

Metric/U.K.		U.S.
100g/¼lb	Sugar	½ cup
450ml/¾ pint	Water	2 cups
1	Vanilla pod	1
	Large peaches, peeled,	
	halved and stoned	
2	(pitted)	2
	Double (heavy) cream	
75ml/3floz	stiffly whipped	⅓ cup
	Fresh raspberries,	
6	chilled	6
1 Tbsp	Flaked almonds	1 Tbsp
MELBA SAUCE		
100g/¼lb	Fresh raspberries	¼lb
	Icing (confectioners')	
25g/1oz	sugar	¼ cup

In a large saucepan dissolve sugar in water over low heat, stirring constantly. When sugar has dissolved add vanilla pod, increase heat to moderate and bring syrup to the boil. Reduce heat to low and simmer for 3 minutes. Remove vanilla pod. Place peaches in syrup, cut sides up, and poach for 5 minutes. Set aside to cool. Transfer peaches and syrup to a shallow bowl and chill in the refrigerator for 1 hour.

Meanwhile, make the sauce. Rub the raspberries through a strainer into a bowl. Discard contents of strainer. Stir sugar into raspberry purée.

Place peaches in 2 individual serving dishes. Reserve syrup for another recipe. Spoon sauce over peaches. Pipe cream, using a forcing bag and star nozzle, around the edge. Decorate with the whole raspberries and sprinkle with almonds. Serve at once.

ORANGE BASKETS

Orange baskets are more of a garnish for a dessert, rather than an actual dessert. They can be served filled with fresh fruit and cream, but also look very effective filled with chopped cooked vegetables and served at a buffet table.

Metric/U.K.		U.S.
2	Large oranges	2

Cut a thin slice from the stalk end of each orange so that it will stand firm. Draw the shape of a basket with a handle on the orange. With a very sharp knife, carefully cut out peel and flesh between the handle and top of the basket. Run the knife under the handle and remove flesh and membrane. With a grapefruit knife, scoop out the remaining flesh and membrane from the inside of the basket. Scrape out any remaining flesh or pith from the basket. It is now ready to use.

An alternative method is to cut the

orange in half then scoop out flesh and membrane from both halves. Carefully cut a small strip (for the handle) from the half without the flat base. Discard remaining rind. Make 2 small holes either side in both the flat-based orange half and the handle strip at the ends. Use 2 long-stemmed cloves to attach the handle to the basket.

ORANGES WITH CINNAMON

Metric/U.K.		U.S.
	Large oranges, peeled	
2	and pith removed	2
1 tsp	Sugar	1 tsp
¼ tsp	Ground cinnamon	¼ tsp
1 Tbsp	Orange liqueur	1 Tbsp

Slice the oranges very thinly, crossways. It is best to do this over a bowl so that you do not lose any juice.

Place orange slices and juice in individual serving dishes. Sprinkle with sugar, cinnamon and liqueur. Chill in the refrigerator for 30 minutes before serving.

ADAM AND EVE PUDDING

Metric/U.K.		U.S.
	Tart, medium dessert	
	apples, peeled cored,	
3	and sliced	3
¼ tsp	Ground cinnamon	¼ tsp
4 Tbsp	Cold water	4 Tbsp
7 Tbsp	Sugar	7 Tbsp
75g/3oz	Butter, softened	⅓ cup
75g/3oz	Self-raising flour	¾ cup
1	Egg, lightly beaten	1

Preheat the oven to 180°C/350°F (gas mark 4). Arrange the apples in a small pie dish. Sprinkle with cinnamon, 2 Tbsp of the water and 1 Tbsp of the sugar. Set aside.

Cream the remaining sugar and the butter together in a bowl. Add beaten egg, a little at a time, beating well after each addition, then beat in the remaining water. Sift flour into bowl and gently but thoroughly fold into the mixture. Spoon mixture over apples, smoothing over the top. Bake for 30 minutes. Reduce oven temperature to 150°C /300°F (gas mark 2) and bake for a further 15 minutes. Serve at once.

Adam and Eve Pudding

BLACKBERRY FOOL

Any soft fruit may be used instead of blackberries.

Metric/U.K.		U.S.
¼kg/½lb	Blackberries	½lb
2 Tbsp	Water	2 Tbsp
75g/3oz	Sugar	⅓ cup
	Double (heavy) cream	
150ml/¼ pint	chilled	⅔ cup

Put the blackberries, water and sugar into a saucepan and bring to the boil over moderate heat. Reduce heat to low, cover and stew for 30 minutes.

Rub the blackberry mixture through a strainer into a bowl. Discard contents of strainer. Leave to cool. Beat cream until thick.

Fold blackberries into cream and spoon into individual dishes. Chill in the refrigerator for 1 hour before serving.

BAKED BANANAS

Metric/U.K.		U.S.
25g/1oz	Butter	2 Tbsp
2 Tbsp	Soft (light) brown sugar	2 Tbsp
a pinch	Ground cloves	a pinch
a pinch	Ground ginger	a pinch
1 Tbsp	Fresh orange juice	1 Tbsp

Right: *Plum Tricorns*

Metric/U.K.		U.S.
1 tsp	Lemon juice	1 tsp
2	Bananas, sliced in half lengthways	2

Preheat the oven to 190°C/375°F (gas mark 5).

In a small bowl, cream the butter and sugar together. Beat in cloves, ginger, orange and lemon juice. Arrange bananas in a greased baking dish and spread with butter and sugar mixture.

Bake for 10 minutes. Remove from oven and serve at once.

PLUM TRICORNS

Metric/U.K.		U.S.
4	Plums, halved and stoned (pitted)	4
4 tsp	Caster (superfine) sugar	4 tsp
100g/¼lb	Shortcrust pastry (see page 13)	¼lb
4 Tbsp	Single (light) cream	4 Tbsp
GLAZE		
	Milk	
	Caster (superfine) sugar	

Preheat the oven to 200°C/400°F (gas mark 6).

Fill the cavity of 4 plum halves with sugar, then sandwich together with other halves.

Roll out the pastry on a floured board to a rectangle 15 x 12.5 cm/6 x 5 inches. To make guidelines for cutting out triangles, fold strip in half and unfold. Then fold both ends of strip to centre crease and unfold back to original position. Cut strip in to 3 equal triangles by cutting diagonally up and down. Join 2 half triangles together, dampening edges, to make another triangle.

To make guidelines for each tricorn, take each point of triangle up to its opposite corner. Unfold after each fold.

Brush outside edges with water and place a plum in the centre of each triangle. Bring up each corner to make a pyramid shape. Seal firmly together. Fold back tips of pastry to make a hole. Transfer to a baking tray, brush with milk, then sprinkle with sugar. Put into oven and bake for 30 minutes.

Just before serving, dribble a little cream into each tricorn and sprinkle with more caster (superfine) sugar.

Gooseberry Crumble

LEMON BREAD PUDDING

An elegant way of using up all that stale bread you didn't know what to do with.

Metric/U.K.		U.S.
	Large slices stale white bread, crusts removed and generously	
4	buttered	4
2 Tbsp	Flaked almonds	2 Tbsp
25g/1oz	Mixed candied peel	⅙ cup
¼ tsp	Mixed spice	¼ tsp
1	Grated zest of lemon	1
1½ Tbsp	Soft (light) brown sugar	1½ Tbsp
CUSTARD		
2	Eggs (small)	2
¼ tsp	Vanilla extract	¼ tsp
2 or 3		2 or 3
drops	Almond extract	drops
300ml/½ pint	Milk	1¼ cups
1 Tbsp	Sugar	1 Tbsp

Preheat the oven to 190°C/375°F (gas mark 5). Cut the bread into quarters and arrange, buttered sides, up, in a shallow baking dish. Make alternate layers with the remaining ingredients, finishing with bread.

For the custard, beat the eggs and extracts together in a bowl. Heat the milk and sugar together over moderate heat and stir until sugar has dissolved. Gradually pour milk on to egg mixture, stirring constantly. Pour custard through a strainer on to bread mixture in dish. Set aside for 15 minutes to allow the bread to soak up the liquid.

Bake for 35 minutes or until golden. Serve at once.

GOOSEBERRY CRUMBLE

Metric/U.K.		U.S.
350g/¾lb	Gooseberries, trimmed	¾lb
50g/2oz	Sugar	¼ cup
1 Tbsp	Water	1 Tbsp
CRUMBLE		
100g/¼lb	Flour	1 cup
50g/2oz	Butter	¼ cup
50g/2oz	Soft (light) brown sugar	¼ cup
2 Tbsp	Walnuts finely chopped	2 Tbsp

Preheat the oven to 200°C/400°F (gas mark 6). For the crumble, sift flour into a bowl and rub in butter until mixture resembles fine breadcrumbs. Stir in sugar and walnuts.

Arrange the gooseberries in a greased baking dish and sprinkle with sugar and water. Cover gooseberries with crumble mixture. Bake for 40 minutes. Serve at once.

MINCEMEAT PIES

You don't have to wait until Christmas to enjoy these little pies. Instead of the smaller circles, cut out star shapes and use to cover the mincemeat.

Metric/U.K.		U.S.
175g/6oz	Shortcrust pastry (see page 13)	6oz
8 tsp	Mincemeat	8 tsp
1½ Tbsp	Milk	1½ Tbsp
	Caster (superfine) sugar	

Preheat the oven to 200°C/400°F (gas mark 6).

Roll out the pastry on a floured surface to 6 mm/¼ inch thick. Cut out eight 7.5 cm/3 inch circles and use to line 8 greased patty tins. Spoon a little of the mincemeat into each tin and dampen edges of pastry.

Cut out eight 6 cm/2½ inch circles and use to cover mincemeat. Crimp edges to seal. Brush with milk. Bake for 20 minutes. Transfer to a serving dish, sprinkle with caster (superfine) sugar and serve.

CHERRY PIE

Metric/U.K.		U.S.
½kg/1lb	Canned stoned (pitted) morello cherries	1lb

1½ Tbsp	Sugar	1½ Tbsp
2 or 3 drops	Vanilla extract	2 or 3 drops
½ Tbsp	Cornflour (cornstarch)	½ Tbsp
175g/6oz	Shortcrust pastry (see page 13)	6oz
1	Small egg white, lightly beaten	1
	Caster (superfine)sugar	

Preheat the oven to 190°C/375°F (gas mark 5).

Drain cherries, reserving 6 Tbsp of syrup from can. Bring syrup, sugar and vanilla extract to the boil in a small saucepan over moderate heat. Add cherries and cook for 1 minute. Remove from heat and stir in cornflour (cornstarch). Stir until dissolved and set aside to cool.

Divide dough into 2 unequal pieces. Roll

Mincemeat Pies

out larger piece of dough on a floured surface and use to line a (15 cm) 6 in greased pie dish. Spoon in cherry filling.

Roll out remaining piece of dough to a circle slightly larger than the rim of the dish. Cover the filling. Dampen edges, trim and crimp to seal. Make 2 slits in the top of the pastry. Brush with egg white and sprinkle with caster (superfine) sugar. Bake for 30 minutes.

Serve at once.

RECRUITMENT APPLE PASTRIES

Metric/U.K.		U.S.
100g/¼lb	Shortcrust pastry (see page 13)	¼lb
2	Large tart dessert apples, peeled and cored	2
100g/¼lb	Canned tropical fruit salad, drained	¼lb
1 Tbsp	Sugar	1 Tbsp
¼ tsp	Ground cinnamon	¼ tsp

Preheat the oven to 200°C/400°F (gas mark 6).

Roll out the dough on a floured surface to a large rectangle. Cut dough into 2 equal squares, reserving trimmings. Place an apple in the centre of each square and fill the cavity with fruit salad. Sprinkle with half the sugar and the cinnamon.

Dampen edges and bring them up to completely enclose apples. Pinch edges to seal. Cut out leaf shapes from trimmings, dampen and press on to pastry. Place apples on a greased baking sheet and sprinkle with remaining sugar. Bake for 30 minutes. Serve at once.

MERINGUES

These are made from meringue cuite, a cooked meringue mixture which holds its shape well when piped. The mixture will make about eighteen 5 cm/2 in meringues. Store in an airtight container for up to one week.

Metric/U.K.		U.S.
4	Egg whites	4
small pinch	Salt	small pinch
Icing (confectioners')		
275g/10oz	sugar, sifted	2 cups
3 drops	Vanilla extract	3 drops

Line a baking sheet with greaseproof (waxed) paper and brown paper with a little oil.

Preheat the oven to 110°C/225°F (gas mark ¼).

Place egg whites in a heatproof bowl and stir in salt. Whisk until foamy but not stiff. Whisk in sugar, 1 tsp at a time. Whisk in vanilla extract.

Place bowl over a saucepan of simmering water and whisk until mixture thickens. This will take about 8 minutes.

Fill a forcing bag fitted with a large star nozzle with the meringue mixture. Pipe small lengths on to prepared baking sheet. Bake for 1½ hours.

When cooked, removed from paper and cool on wire rack.

LEMON MERINGUE PIE

Metric/U.K.		U.S.
	Shortcrust pastry (see	
100g/¼lb	page 13)	¼lb
FILLING		
	Grated zest and juice	
1½	of lemons	1½
150ml/¼ pint	Water	⅔ cup
	Caster (superfine)	
2 Tbsp	sugar	2 Tbsp
1½ Tbsp	Arrowroot, dissolved	1½ Tbsp
	in 1 Tbsp water	
2	Egg yolks, lightly beaten	2
MERINGUE		
2	Egg whites	2
	Caster (superfine)	
75g/3oz	sugar	⅓ cup

Preheat the oven to 200°C/400°F (gas mark 6). Line a 15 cm/6 inch flan dish with the pastry and chill in the refrigerator for 15 minutes. Cover base with greaseproof (waxed) paper and baking beans. Bake blind for 10 minutes. Remove paper and beans and set aside.

For the filling, combine lemon zest and juice, water and sugar in a pan. Cook, stirring, over moderate heat until sugar has dissolved. Stir in dissolved arrowroot and continue cooking for 5 minutes, stirring, until thick. Allow mixture to cool, then beat in egg yolks. Spoon mixture into the pastry case. Reduce oven temperature to 180°C/350°F (gas mark 4) and bake filling for 5 minutes.

For the meringue, beat the egg whites until frothy then gradually beat in sugar. Continue beating until mixture forms stiff peaks. Pile on top of filling to cover completely.

Bake for 20 minutes.

Serve at once.

Recruitment Apple Pastries

INDEX